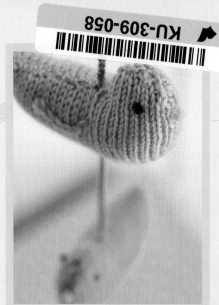

my first
ANIMAL KNITTING
BOOK

30 fantastic knits for children aged 7+

FIONA GOBLE

CICO **Kidz**

Published in 2019 by CICO Books
An imprint of Ryland Peters & Small Ltd
20–21 Jockey's Fields, London WC1R 4BW
341 E 116th St, New York, NY 10029

www.rylandpeters.com

10 9 8 7 6 5 4 3 2 1

A CIP catalog record for this book is available from
the Library of Congress and the British Library.

ISBN: 978 1 78249 707 3

Printed in China

Series consultant: Susan Akass
Editor: Gillian Haslam
Designer: Alison Fenton
Illustrator: Rachel Boulton
Character illustrations: Hannah George

In-house editor: Dawn Bates
In-house designer: Eliana Holder
Art director: Sally Powell
Production controller: David Hearn
Publishing manager: Penny Craig
Publisher: Cindy Richards

For photography credits, see page 128.

Contents

Introduction

If knitting plain squares isn't your thing, how about some cute but easy knitted animals? There are all sorts of wooly creature knits inside this book, including accessories like a fox scarf and kitten bag, and stuff to make for your room or as gifts for friends. Who wouldn't love a bunny pillow or a piglet hot water bottle cozy? And there's even an adorable knitted aardvark!

These projects are written for someone who has already caught the knitting bug and has learnt the basics of knitting, but they also introduce some extra techniques which will mean that you can shape your knitting in new ways and create these wonderful animal designs. All these extras are explained in the Techniques section, but they are easier to understand if somebody also shows you how to do them. So search out a keen knitter—a family member, a friend, or even the person who runs your local yarn store. They would probably be delighted to pass on their skills to a new knitter.

At the beginning of each project there's a list of the knitting tools and yarn you need to complete that item. There are also illustrated steps showing exactly what you need to do. Whatever item you choose, read the instructions carefully before you begin to make sure you understand everything and feel confident. If there's anything you're unsure about, check out the Techniques section on pages 9–23, which explains all you need to know. Knitting patterns are written using special abbreviations, some of which you probably know already. If there's anything you don't understand, take a look at the Abbreviations section on page 23 where you can find out what everything means.

The book contains 30 projects, divided into three sections: Barnyard Animals is full of projects starring creatures from the farm or countryside homes, including some speckled hen egg cozies and a marmalade kitten scarf.

Woodland Creatures features cute beasties like birds, mice, and ducklings. There's even a cool cozy for your recorder in the shape of a snake.

The Wildlife chapter includes knits inspired by elephants, pandas, seals, sharks, and more. So head here if you fancy a zebra cowl or perhaps a koala book cozy. There are differing skill levels (see the key opposite).

Have fun deciding which items to make. Choose your own colors, add your own twists, and let your imagination run free!

Project levels

☺ ○ ○

Level 1

These are quick, easy
projects that use basic
knitting stitches.

☺ ☺ ○

Level 2

These projects take
a little longer
and use more
advanced techniques.

☺ ☺ ☺

Level 3

These may have several
stages and require more
difficult knitting and
sewing techniques.

Materials

You need just two items to start your animal knits: a pair of needles and a ball of yarn. There are also a few other bits and pieces you'll need to make some of the projects in this book, but none of them are expensive and you'll probably have some of them at home already.

- **Knitting needles**
  Needles come in different materials and sizes. Each pattern tells you the size you will need to make the project.

- **Pompom maker**
  This little gadget offers a quick and easy way to make pompoms used to decorate some knitting projects (or you can use cardboard rings, as shown on page 20).

- **Scissors**
  Always cut your yarn, don't try to break it, even when the pattern says "break yarn," as strong yarn will cut your hand.

- **Stitch marker**
  For marking your place in your knitting when you need to return to complete the stitches. You can use a small safety pin or a piece of contrasting thread.

- **Buttons**
  Use buttons to add decoration or fastenings to your knitting. Snap fasteners are also used in some projects.

- **Sewing needle and thread**
  For sewing on buttons.

- **Embroidery needle**
  For embroidering details, such as eyes.

- **Yarn sewing/darning needle**
  Large, blunt needles with big eyes that can be threaded with yarn for sewing up knitting.

- **Crochet hook**
  This is needed for making crochet chains or edgings and is also useful for picking up dropped stitches.

- **Pins**
  Thick pins are best for holding bits of knitting together when you sew them up.

- **Fiberfill toy stuffing**
  For turning your knitted items into soft toys or filling out shapes.

YARNS

The projects give you the brand and type of yarn we used, but if you can't find an exact match, you will still be able to knit using a similar type of yarn (for example, light worsted/DK or bulky/chunky) made up of similar fibers (e.g. 100% wool). You will need to check that the yarn you want to use has the same recommended needle size and gauge (tension) and that the length of yarn per ball is the same. This information is given in every pattern, and on the band around the ball, or on websites that sell yarn. You can also try the Yarnsub website for suggestions: www.yarnsub.com.

Knitting Techniques

Getting started

Holding the needles

The two most common ways of holding the needles are like a pen or like a knife. You can hold each needle in the same way, or have each hand use a different way. Even if you are left-handed you can knit like this, as both hands do some work. In the drawing, the left hand is holding the needle like a knife, and the right hand is holding the needle like a pen.

Holding the yarn

The yarn you are working with needs to be held properly to produce an evenly knitted fabric. Try the methods shown here to find out which suits you best.

Yarn in right hand: To knit and purl in the English/American style (see pages 10 and 11), hold the yarn in your right hand. To hold the yarn tightly (above left), wind it right around your little finger, under your ring and middle fingers, then pass it over your index finger; this finger will manipulate the yarn. For a looser hold (above right), catch the yarn between your little and ring fingers, pass it under your middle finger, then over your index finger.

Yarn in left hand: To knit and purl in the continental style (see pages 11 and 12), hold the yarn in your left hand. To hold the yarn tightly (above left), wind it right around your little finger, under your ring and middle fingers, then pass it over your index finger; this finger will manipulate the yarn. For a looser hold (above right), fold your little, ring, and middle fingers over the yarn, and wind it twice around your index finger.

Slip knot

The first step when starting to knit is to make a slip knot, which will also be your first stitch.

1 With the ball of yarn to your right, lay the end of the yarn on the palm of your left hand. With your right hand, wind the yarn twice round your index and middle  fingers to make a loop. Make a second loop behind the first one. Slip a knitting needle in front of the first loop to pick up the second loop.

2 Slip the yarn off your fingers leaving the loop on the needle. Gently pull on both yarn ends to tighten the knot a little, then pull on the strand of yarn leading to the ball to fully tighten the knot on the needle.

Casting on

There are many ways to cast on, but for beginners this is the simplest way. Use this technique to start with—you can progress to something harder once you have mastered knitting.

1 Make a slip knot on the needle and pull on the ends of the yarn to make the slip knot tight on the needle. You have made your first stitch.

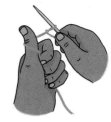

2 Holding the needle in your right hand, make a loop around your left thumb with the ball-end of the yarn. Slip the needle under the loop.

3 Remove your thumb and pull the stitch tight on the needle. Add on as many stitches as you need in the same way.

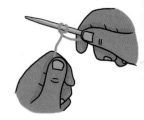

Knitting stitches

Once you have cast on, there are only two basic stitches to learn, knit stitch and purl stitch. The aim is to hold the needle with the stitches on in your left hand and the empty needle in your right hand, and to transfer all stitches onto the right-hand needle by knitting a row. Most people in the English-speaking world knit using a method called English (or American) knitting. However, in parts of Europe, people prefer a method known as Continental knitting.

Knit stitch

This is the simpler of the stitches.

Knit stitch English/American style

1 Hold the needle with the cast-on stitches in your left hand and the empty needle in your right hand. From left to right, put the tip of the right-hand needle into the front of the first stitch on the left-hand needle. Wrap the yarn coming from the ball around the point of the right-hand needle with your right hand, passing the yarn underneath then over the point of the right-hand needle.

2 With the tip of the right needle, pull the wrapped yarn through the stitch on the left-hand needle to form a loop on the right-hand needle. This loop is your new stitch.

3 Slip the loop off the left-hand needle to complete the stitch, which is now on your right-hand needle. Repeat these steps with each stitch, until all the stitches on the left-hand needle have been knitted and transferred to the right-hand needle. This completes the row. To start a new row, swap the needles in your hands so that the needle with the stitches is in your left hand and the yarn coming from the ball is in position at the start of the row.

Knit stitch Continental style

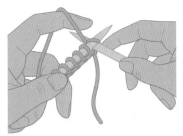 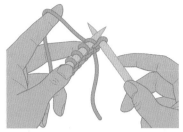 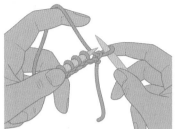

1 Hold the needle with the stitches to be knitted in your left hand and then insert the tip of the right-hand needle into the front of the first stitch on the left-hand needle, from left to right. Holding the yarn fairly taut with your left hand at the back of your work, use the tip of the right-hand needle to pick up a loop of yarn.

2 With the tip of the right-hand needle, bring the yarn through the original stitch to form a loop. This loop is the new stitch.

3 Slip the original stitch off the left-hand needle by gently pulling the right-hand needle to the right. Repeat these steps until you have knitted all the stitches on the left-hand needle.
To work the next row, transfer the needle with all the stitches into your left hand.

Purl stitch

This stitch is almost as simple as knit stitch. You still hold the needle with stitches in your left hand, but you insert the right-hand needle a different way into each stitch and you hold the yarn at the front.

Purl stitch English/American style

1 Hold the needle with the cast-on stitches in your left hand. Insert the tip of the right-hand needle into the front of the first stitch on the left-hand needle, from right to left. Holding the ball-end of the yarn at the front of the knitting, wrap this yarn around the point of the right-hand needle with your right hand, passing the yarn over and around the right-hand needle.

2 With the tip of the right needle, pull the yarn through the stitch on the left-hand needle to form a loop.

3 Slip the loop off the left-hand needle to complete the stitch, which is now on your right-hand needle. Repeat these steps with each stitch, until all the stitches on the left-hand needle have been transferred to the right-hand needle. This completes the row. To start a new row, swap the needles in your hands so that the needle with the stitches is in your left hand and the yarn is in position at the start of the row.

Purl stitch Continental style

1 Hold the needle with the stitches to be knitted in your left hand and then insert the tip of the right-hand needle into the front of the first stitch on the left-hand needle, from right to left. Holding the yarn fairly taut at the front of the work, move the tip of the right-hand needle under the working yarn, then push your left index finger downward, as shown, to hold the yarn around the needle.

2 With the tip of the right-hand needle, bring the yarn through the original stitch to form a loop.

3 Slip the original stitch off the left-hand needle by gently pulling the right-hand needle to the right. Repeat these steps until you have purled all the stitches on the left-hand needle. To work the next row, transfer the needle with all the stitches into your left hand.

Bind (cast) off and fastening off

When you have finished knitting you need to bind (cast) off so that your work doesn't just unravel! To bind (cast) off purlwise, follow the instructions below, but purl the stitches rather than knit them.

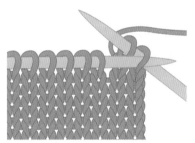

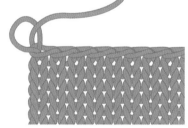

1 First knit two stitches (see page 10). Slip the tip of your left-hand needle into the first stitch knitted, lift it over the stitch closest to the tip of the needle and drop it off the needle. Make sure the other stitch stays on the needle. Knit one more stitch onto the right-hand needle again, and repeat until all you have left is one stitch on the right-hand needle. All the other stitches have been bound (cast) off.

2 Slip the last stitch off the needle, pull it out a bit to make it bigger, then cut off the yarn, leaving a long tail. Slip the tail through the loop of the last stitch then pull on the tail to tighten the loop and finish the bind (cast) off. This is called fastening off.

Binding (casting) off in rib
You can also bind (cast) off in rib if you have been using that stitch for the fabric, as it will give you a neat and stretchy edge. To do this, cast (bind) off as normal, simply working across the stitches in the rib pattern (knit 1, purl 1) you have been working, rather than knitting all of them.

Stitch patterns

Depending on how you combine knit and purl stitches, you can make various stitch patterns to produce knitted fabrics that feel and look very different.

Garter stitch

Knitting every row forms a ridged fabric called garter stitch, which is the simplest stitch pattern. It is the same on both sides and so is a flat, even fabric that is perfect for scarves or edges.

Seed (moss) stitch

Seed (moss) stitch is made by working alternate knit and purl stitches across the same row. As you hold the yarn at the back for knit stitches and at the front for purl stitches, you need to move it after each stitch. After a knit stitch you must pass the yarn in between the needles to the front of the knitting to work the next purl stitch.

After a purl stitch you must pass the yarn in between the needles to the back to make the next knit stitch. In each row you knit the stitches that were knitted in the last row, and purl those that were purled to create the bumpy texture.

Stockinette (stocking) stitch

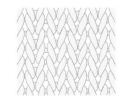

This is made by alternately working one row of knit stitch and one row of purl stitch. This makes a fabric that is different on each side. The knit, or plain, side is flat and the stitches look like little "V"s. The purl side is bumpy and textured, with the stitches like little wiggles.

Rib stitch

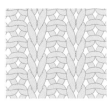

Rib stitch is created like seed (moss) stitch by working knits and purls alternately across a row. But in each following row, you knit the stitches that were purled in the previous row and purl the stitches that were knitted, to make the vertical stripes of stitches.

Double rib

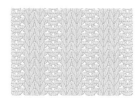

This is made using the same principle as single rib, but you work two knit stitches followed by two purl stitches across each row.

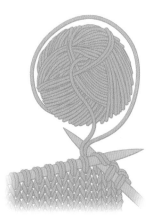

Knitting with two yarns held together

Some of the patterns will tell you to knit with two strands of yarn at the same time (doubled). Where you are using two different yarns, as in the Duckling Scarf (see page 41), you can just take the end of each ball and hold both yarns together. Where you are using two strands of the same yarn, you can take one end from the outside of the ball, and the other end from inside the middle of the ball. Take care to pick up each strand as you knit or purl into them together.

Gauge (tension)

Gauge (tension) is the tightness or looseness of your knitting. The gauge will affect the size of your finished piece. For some of the patterns in this book you do not have to worry too much about gauge as it doesn't really matter how big or small the final project is. However, when you are getting really good at knitting and begin trying some of the Level 3 hat patterns, gauge does matter because your finished hat could be too big or too small if it is wrong.

Before you begin your project you need to knit a gauge (tension) swatch. This is a small square knitted in the yarn and needle size given in the gauge (tension) section for your chosen pattern, in stockinette (stocking) stitch. You will need to add a few stitches on rows, so if the pattern says "15sts and 20 rows ... to a 4-in (10-cm) square," cast on 20 stitches, and knit 24 rows. When you have bound (cast) off, lay the knitting flat, place a ruler on it, and mark out

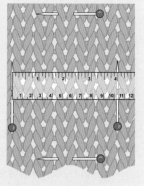

(with pins) a square that is 4 x 4in (10 x 10cm). Count the number of stitches and rows in the marked-out square.

If you find you have more stitches or rows per 4in (or 10cm) than asked for in the pattern, then your gauge is too tight. To make it looser, try a bigger size of knitting needle—knit another swatch and check again. Increase the size of the needle you use until the gauge is as close as you can get it to the one you need for the pattern.

If there are not enough stitches or rows in the square, then your gauge is too loose, and you need to try smaller knitting needles.

It is more important to have the right number of stitches than the right number of rows.

Shaping

To shape a knitted piece, you have to increase or decrease the number of stitches on the needles. Here are the simplest ways.

Increasing

Increase (inc)
This is also known as knitting twice into a stitch, or knit into front and back.

Increasing on a purl row (inc purlwise)

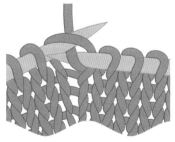

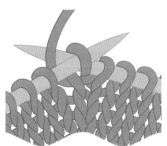

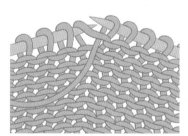

1 Knit into the front of the next stitch on the left-hand needle in the normal way, but do not slip it off the needle.

2 With the stitch still on the left-hand needle and the yarn at the back, knit into the back of the same stitch and then slip it off the needle. You have made one stitch into two stitches and so increased by one.

1 Purl the next stitch on the left-hand needle in the usual way, but do not slip the "old" stitch off the left-hand needle.

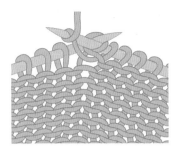

2 Twist the right-hand needle backward to make it easier to put it into the same stitch again, but through the back of the stitch this time. Purl the stitch again, then slip the "old" stitch off the left-hand needle in the usual way.

Make 1 stitch (m1)

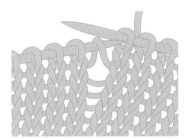

1 From the front, slip the tip of the left-hand needle under the horizontal strand of yarn running between the last stitch on the right-hand needle and the first stitch on the left-hand needle.

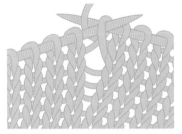

2 Put the right-hand needle knitwise into the back of the loop formed by the picked-up strand and knit the back of the loop in the same way you would knit a stitch. You have made 1 stitch.

Decreasing

This means reducing the number of stitches, to shape your knitting. There are various ways to do this.

Knit 2 stitches together (k2tog)

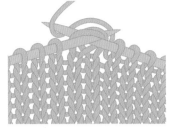

1 Instead of inserting your right-hand needle into the front of the first stitch on the left-hand needle, insert it into the second stitch and then into the first stitch as well. Then knit the two stitches together, and slide both from the left-hand needle. You have made two stitches into one. To knit three stitches together—k3tog—put the needle through three stitches and knit three together.

Purl 2 stitches together (p2tog)

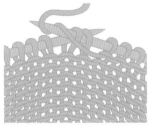

Simply insert your needle through two stitches instead of one when you begin your stitch and then purl them in the normal way. To purl three stitches together—p3tog—put the needle into three stitches and purl all three together.

Knit two together through back loop (k2togtbl)

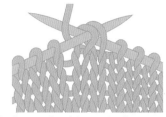

This is worked in a similar way to k2tog, but instead of inserting the right needle into the stitches from front to back, you insert it from right to left, through the back of the two stitches, and then you knit them together.

Slip slip knit (ssk)

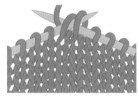

Slip one stitch and then the next stitch onto your right-hand needle without knitting them. Then insert the left-hand needle from left to right through the front loops of both the slipped stitches and knit them as normal.

Slip one, knit one, pass the slipped stitch over (sl1, k1, psso)

Slip the first stitch knitwise from the left-hand needle to the right-hand needle without knitting it. Knit the next stitch, then lift the slipped stitch over the knitted stitch and drop it off the needle.

Joining in a new ball or a new color

When you run out of a ball of yarn, you need to add a new ball at the beginning of a row. You will also usually bring in a new color (as directed in the pattern) at the beginning of a row.

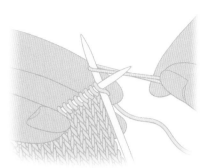

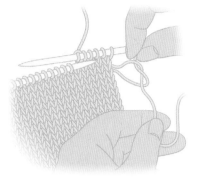

1 Break the old yarn, leaving a 4–6in (10–15cm) tail. Insert the needle into the next stitch to be knitted, then knit it in the new color as usual, leaving a 4–6in (10–15cm) tail of the new color yarn.

2 Knit a few more stitches in the new color, then tie the tails together with a single knot to stop the loose first stitch falling off the needle. Don't use a double knot as this will make it difficult to sew the ends in later, and the knot will eventually work itself out of the knitting.

Carrying yarn up the side of the work

When you knit stripe patterns, you do not need to join in a new color for every stripe. Instead, carry the color not in use up the side of the work until you need it again.

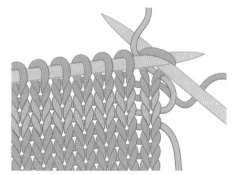

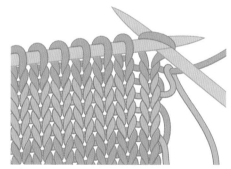

1 If the stripes change every two rows, then just bring the yarn not in use up and knit with it as needed.

2 If the stripes are wider, then you need to catch in the yarn not in use at the ends of rows to prevent long, loose strands appearing. To do this, put the right-hand needle into the first stitch of a row, lay the yarn to be carried over the working yarn and then knit the stitch in the working yarn.

Knitting in two colors

This is the method of color knitting for patterns that go over a whole row (like the Rattlesnake Scarf on page 93). If you haven't done it before, then it's a good idea to try it out on swatches before starting a project, as getting the gauge (tension) of the yarns right can take a bit of practice.

Changing color on a knit row

It's important to swap the yarns in the right way when changing colors to keep the fabric flat and smooth.

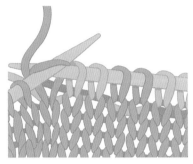

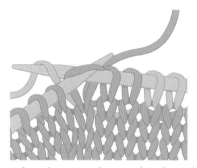

1 Knit the stitches in color A (brown in this example), bringing the yarn across over the strand of color B (lime in this example) to wrap around the needle.

2 At the color change, drop color A and pick up color B, bringing across under the strand of color A to wrap around the needle. Be careful not to pull it too tight. Knit the stitches in color B. When you change it back to color A, bring it across over the strand of color B.

Changing color on a purl row

You can clearly see how the colors are swapped when working the purl rows.

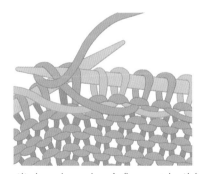

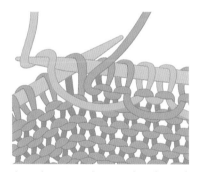

1 Purl the stitches in color A (brown in this example), bringing the yarn across over the strand of color B (lime in this example) to wrap around the needle.

2 At the color change, drop color A and pick up color B, bringing it across under the strand of color A to wrap around the needle. Be careful not to pull it too tight. Purl the stitches in color B. When you change back to color A, bring it across over the strand of color B.

Picking up stitches

Sometimes you need to pick up stitches along the side or top of a piece you have already knitted, to add legs or feet for example. Always do this with the right side of the knitting facing you and try to space the stitches you pick up at equal intervals.

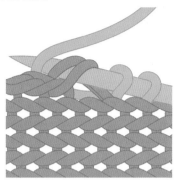

1 Hold the needle in your right hand and put it through the end of a row where you want to pick up a stitch. Wrap a new piece of yarn around the needle, and pull the loop through the knitted fabric to the front. Continue in this way along the edge until you have picked up enough stitches.

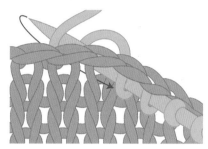

2 If you need to pick up stitches at the top or bottom (the cast-on or bound-/or cast-off edge), put your needle into the stitches, rather than the gaps between rows.

Picking up dropped stitches

Sometimes a stitch will accidentally slip off your needle before it is knitted and will create a space, or a ladder, in your knitting. You can pick up the dropped stitch using a crochet hook.

   With the knitting facing you, knit to where there is a gap left by the dropped stitch. Insert a crochet hook from the front to the back through the dropped stitch and hook it behind the strand of the "ladder" above it. Pull the ladder through the stitch with the hook. Keep hooking the ladders until you reach the top, then slip the loop onto the left-hand needle, and knit it as normal.

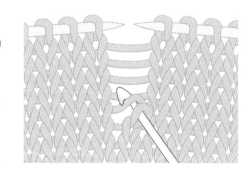

Weaving in yarn ends

When you have finished a piece of knitting (especially a stripy one), you will have lots of untidy tails of yarn loose at the edges. It is important to weave these into your knitting to make it tidy and secure. You can't just cut them off or your knitting will unravel. Always weave in any ends when you have finished your knitting.

To weave them in, thread a darning needle with one of the tails of yarn. On the wrong side, take the needle through the knitting one stitch along from the edge, then weave it through the stitches, without letting your needle go through to the right side, working in a gentle zigzag. Work through 4 or 5 stitches, then return in the opposite direction. Remove the needle, pull the knitting gently to stretch it, and trim the end.

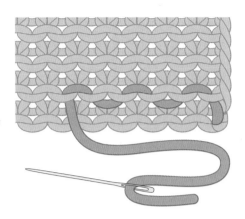

Sewing up

Sewing up knitting can be done in many ways, but oversewing is the easiest. For each method thread a yarn sewing needle with a long piece of yarn.

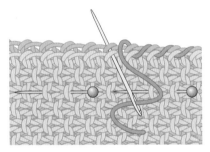

Oversewing
This can be used to join seams, or to sew pieces on to your knitting (such as ears). Secure the yarn to one piece of knitting with a few little stitches on the back. For a seam, lay the pieces to be joined with right sides together. Insert the needle into the front of one piece of knitting, then through to the back of the adjoining piece. Bring the yarn over the top of the edges ready for the next stitch. Repeat all along the seam or join.

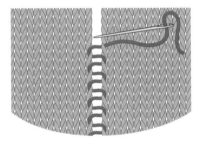

Flat stitch
This is the technique used for sewing up many of the projects in this book. It creates a join that is completely flat. Lay the two edges to be joined side by side, right sides up. Pick up the very outermost strand of knitting from one side and then the other, working your way along the seam and pulling the yarn up firmly every few stitches.

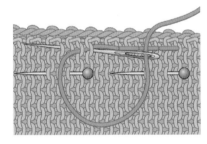

Backstitch
Lay the pieces to be joined right sides together. Insert the needle at the right-hand corner through both pieces of knitting and as close as you can get to the edge, from front to back. Bring the needle back through to the front a little further on. This time, instead of going forward, put the needle back through at the end of your first stitch. Bring it out again a stitch-length ahead of the thread, and repeat. You will have a line of joined-up stitches.

Finishing touches

Sewing on buttons

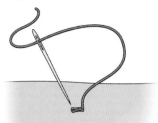

1 Mark the place where you want the button to go. Push the needle up from the back of the fabric and sew a few stitches over and over in this place.

2 Now bring the needle up through one of the holes in the button. Push the needle back down through the second hole and through the fabric. Bring it back up through the first hole. Repeat this five or six times. If there are four holes in the button, use all four of them to make a cross pattern. Keep the stitches close together under the middle of the button. Finish with a few small stitches over and over on the back of the fabric. For snap fasteners, sew a few stitches over and over through each of the four holes on the edge of each fastener half.

Making pompoms

1 Decide the size of your finished pompom. Find a round object with the same diameter and draw around it twice onto a piece of stiff cardstock. Draw a smaller circle inside each larger one (draw around a large button or a cotton reel) exactly in the middle. Cut out the larger circle then cut out the inner circle to make two donut shaped rings.

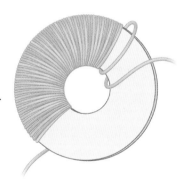

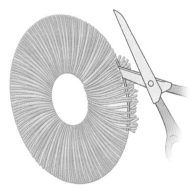

2 Hold the two rings together and wrap the yarn around them and through the center hole, wrapping it closely together. Don't wrap too tightly or it will be difficult to cut. When there are lots of layers of yarn all around the ring, and there is no center hole left, carefully push the point of a pair of scissors through the yarn between the two layers of cardstock. Snip through the layers of yarn all around the ring. Slide a length of yarn between the cardstock rings and tie it tightly with a knot to hold all the strands together. Leave the end of this piece of yarn long for attaching to your projects.

3 Pull off the cardstock rings (you can reuse them for your next pompom) and fluff up the pompom. You can trim any straggly ends with scissors to make a neat ball.

Crochet techniques

While all the projects in this book are knitted, a few of them require simple crochet chains or edging.

Crochet edging

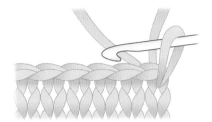  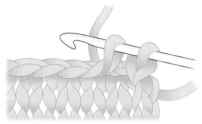

1 A crochet edging can be worked along a horizontal edge or a vertical edge, but the basic technique is the same. Insert the crochet hook in the first space between stitches. Wind the yarn round the hook and pull a loop of yarn through.

2 Wind the yarn round the hook again and then pull the loop through to make a single chain.

3 Insert the hook through the next stitch, wind the yarn round the hook, and pull through a second loop of yarn.

4 Wind the yarn round the hook and pull a loop of yarn through both loops on the hook. Repeat steps 3 and 4, inserting the hook into the spaces between stitches in an even pattern.

For crochet edging along a vertical edge, insert your hook into the spaces between the edges of the rows rather than the spaces between stitches.

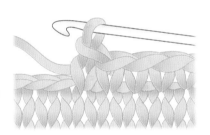

Crochet chain

1 Make a slip knot on the crochet hook in the same way as for knitting (see page 9). Holding the slip knot on the hook, wind the yarn round the hook from the back to front, then catch the yarn in the crochet-hook tip.

2 Pull the yarn through the slip knot of the crochet hook to make the second link in the chain. Continue in this way until the chain is the length needed.

Embroidery Stitches

Running stitch

This is the simplest stitch and is used in the Rabbit Egg Cozies on page 54.

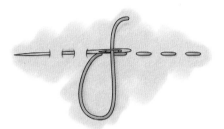

Secure the end of the thread with a few small stitches. Push the needle down through the fabric a little way along, then bring it back up through the fabric a little further along. Repeat to form a row of wide stitches.

Straight stitch

A very easy stitch, often used for whiskers!

Secure the end of the thread with a few small stitches. Take the yarn out at the starting point and back down into the work where you want the stitch to end.

Cross stitch

A very easy, decorative stitch.

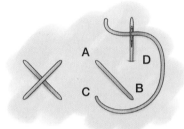

Secure the end of the thread with a few small stitches. Knot your thread, bring the needle up at A and down at B, then up at C and down at D. Knot again at the back or come up in the position of the next cross.

Chain stitch

This is a pretty stitch to learn and you can use it for details such as eyes or teeth.

Bring the yarn out at the starting point on the front of your knitting. Take the needle back into the knitting just next to the starting point, leaving a loop of yarn. Bring the needle out of the knitting again, a stitch length further on, and catch in the loop. To make a ring or line of chain stitches, insert the needle at the point at which it last emerged, just inside the loop of the previous chain, and bring it out a short

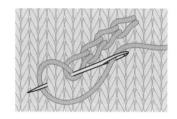

distance away, again looping the thread around the needle tip. Repeat to continue. When you have finished the chain stitch, make a small straight stitch over the end of the loop to hold it in place.

French knot

These little stitches are great for adding pupils to eyes.

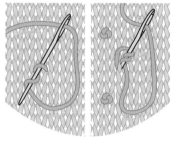

Bring the needle up from the back to the front. Wrap the thread two or three times around the tip of the needle, then reinsert the needle at the point where it first emerged, holding the wrapped threads with the thumbnail of your non-stitching hand, and pull the needle all the way through. The wraps will form a knot on the surface of the fabric.

Following a knitting pattern

To make the projects in this book you will need to follow the patterns. These give instructions on how many and what type of stitches you need. Knitting patterns use abbreviations for the stitches, such as K for knit and P for purl. Patterns combine different numbers of stitches and, sometimes, different types of stitches, to make the shape of the knitted piece.

Knitting patterns are written out as instructions, one row at a time. Start by casting on the number of stitches required and then work each row—remember, your slip knot counts as your first stitch. To help you to keep track of where you are, tick off each row with a pencil when you have completed it. Sometimes the pattern will include the number of stitches that you have made at the end of each row, shown in brackets. Check that your stitches match.

First, practice the basic stitches, how to join in new colors, and how to fasten off, by making a few rectangles of knitting. Once you feel happy that you can work all the different types of stitches, you will be ready to start on your very own project.

Finishing your project will involve some different techniques, from weaving in ends, to sewing up the pieces and sewing on buttons or attaching pompoms. You'll find instructions on how to do this with each project.

Abbreviations

beg	begin/ning
cont	continue
cm	centimeter
dec	decreas(e)(ing)
g	grams
in	inch
inc	increase
k	knit
k2tog	knit 2 stitches together
LH	left hand
m	meter(s)
m1	make 1 stitch
mm	millimeter(s)
oz	ounce(s)
p	purl
p2tog	purl 2 stitches together
psso	pass the slipped stitch over
pwise	purlwise
rem	remaining
RH	right hand
RS	right side
sl	slip
ssk	slip slip knit
st st	stockinette (stocking) stitch
st(s)	stitch(es)
tbl	through back loop
WS	wrong side
yd	yard
[]	work the instructions inside the square brackets for the number of times given
*	work instructions after or between asterisks (stars) as directed.

chapter 1
Barnyard Animals

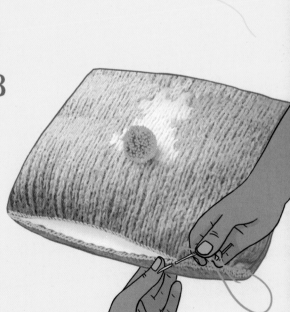

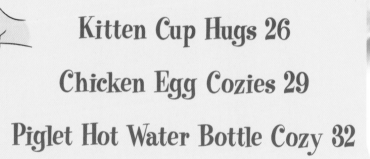

Kitten Cup Hugs

These adorable cup hugs will stop you burning your hands on paper cups when you're out having hot chocolate, and they are a great gift for coffee-loving adults who buy takeouts. Decorate them with a pretty bow.

You will need

For all three cozies:

Patons Merino Extrafine DK (100% wool; 131yd/120m per 1¾oz/50g ball) light worsted (DK) yarn:
1 ball each in shades:
125 Orange (dark orange)
123 Apricot (light orange)
190 Light Grey Heather (gray)
102 Cream (white)

Small oddment of dark gray or black light worsted (DK) yarn for features

A selection of small ready-made ribbon bows, measuring approx. 1¼ x 1¼in (3 x 3cm) or some narrow ribbon to make your own

Sewing thread for sewing on bows

US 3 (3.25mm) knitting needles

Yarn sewing needle

Large-eyed embroidery needle

Standard sewing needle

Gauge (tension)

26 sts and 34 rows in stockinette (stocking) stitch to a 4-in (10-cm) square on US 3 (3.25mm) needles.

Measurements

The finished cozies are 3¾in (9.5cm) across and 1¾in (4.5cm) tall (excluding ears) and will fit a small disposable cup that is 3¾in (9.5cm) tall and has a top circumference of 9¼in (23.5cm).

Abbreviations

k knit
k2tog knit 2 stitches together
kwise knitwise
p purl
pwise purlwise
p2tog purl 2 stitches together
rep repeat
RS right sides
ssk slip slip knit
st(s) stitch(es)
[ ] knit the stitches inside the square brackets as many times as the instructions after the brackets tell you

Techniques

Joining in a new color (see page 16)

Picking up stitches (see page 18)

Shaping (see pages 14–15)

Embroidery stitches (see page 22)

Sewing up (see page 19)

---

1 **For the marmalade kitten cup hug**
Main part
Cast on 47 sts in dark orange. Break the dark orange and join in the light orange.
Row 1: [K1, p1] to last st, k1. Rep row 1, 15 times more. Break light orange and join in dark orange.

Row 17: [K1, p1] to last st, k1. Bind (cast) off kwise.
Make the ears
With RS facing and using dark orange, pick up and knit 6 sts from 15th to 20th stitch along bound- (cast-) off edge.
Row 2: Purl.
Row 3: Ssk, k2, k2tog. *(4 sts)*
Row 4: Purl.

Row 5: Ssk, k2tog. *(2 sts)*
Row 6: P2tog. *(1 st)*
Break yarn and fasten off.
Work the second ear in same way, but from 28th st to 33rd st along bound- (cast-) off edge.

2 **For the gray kitten cup hug**
Work the main part and ears as for marmalade kitten, using gray yarn.
Eye patch
Cast on 5 sts in white.
Row 1: [K1, p1] twice, k1.
Rep row 1, 4 times more.
Bind (cast) off pwise.

3 **For the white kitten cup hug**
Work the main part and ears as for marmalade kitten using white yarn.

Hot drink, COOL hands

4 Add the eye patch
Sew the eye patch onto the gray cozy, following the photograph.

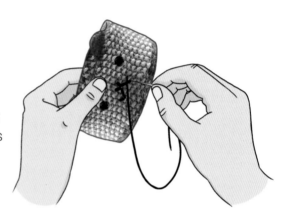

5 Embroider the face
Work a small coil of about 4 chain stitches (see page 22) for the eyes using dark gray or black yarn. Using a divided length of the same yarn, work the noses and mouths using straight stitches (see page 22).

6 Join the sides
Sew the short sides of the cozy together using flat stitch (see page 19).

7 Add the bows
Sew the bows in place using sewing thread. Weave in all loose ends.

Chicken Egg Cozies

What better way to keep your boiled egg warm than to have a cute little knitted chicken sitting on it? These hens are brown, but you can make them as colorful as you wish!

You will need

For both cozies:
Rowan Felted Tweed DK
(50% merino wool, 25% alpaca, 25% viscose; 191yd/175m per 1¾oz/50g ball) light worsted (DK) yarn:
   1 ball each in shades:
   157 Camel (beige)
   154 Ginger (dark orange)

Oddments of red and yellow light worsted (DK) yarns for combs and beaks

Small oddments of off-white and black light worsted (DK) yarns

US 7 (4.5mm) and US 3 (3.25mm) knitting needles

Yarn sewing needle

Large-eyed embroidery needle

Gauge (tension)

16 sts and 27 rows in stockinette (stocking) stitch to a 4-in (10-cm) square on US 7 (4.5mm) needles, using yarn doubled.

Measurements

The finished cozies are 4in (10cm) wide at the widest point, and 3½in (9.5cm) tall to top of comb, and will fit a standard-size egg and egg cup.

Abbreviations

inc increase
k knit
k2tog knit 2 stitches together
m1 make 1 stitch
p purl
p2tog purl 2 stitches together
rem remaining
rep repeat
ssk slip slip knit
st(s) stitches
st st stockinette (stocking) stitch
WS wrong side
* work instructions after or between asterisks (stars) as directed in the pattern

Techniques

Knitting with two yarns held together (see page 13)

Shaping (see pages 14–15)

Embroidery stitches (see page 22)

Sewing up (see page 19)

1 Make the cozy
Side 1

Using US 7 (4.5mm) needles, cast on 14 sts in your chosen color with yarn doubled. Knit 2 rows.
Row 3: Purl.
Row 4 (RS): Inc, k to last 2 sts, inc, k1. (16 sts)
Row 5: Purl.
Row 6: K2, m1, k to last 2 sts, m1, k2. (18 sts)

Beg with a p row, work 7 rows in st st.*
Now begin to shape the head and tail of the hen.
Row 14: K9, bind (cast) off 4 sts, k to end.
Cont working on 5 sts just worked only. The other stitches remain on the needle but you don't knit them.
Next row: Purl.
Next row: Ssk, then using

resulting st bind (cast) off to end. (1 st)
Break yarn and fasten off.
Rejoin yarn to rem sts on WS of work.

Next row: P2tog, p to end. *(8 sts)*

Next row: K to last 2 sts, k2tog. *(7 sts)*

Beg with a p row, work 3 rows in st st.

Next row: Ssk, k3, k2tog. *(5 sts)*

Next row: Purl.

Next row: Ssk, k1, k2tog. *(3 sts)*

Next row: P3tog. *(1 st)*

Break yarn and fasten off.

Side 2

Work as for side 1 to *.

Row 14: K5, bind (cast) off 4 sts, k to end.

Cont working on 9 sts just worked only. The other stitches remain on the needle but you don't knit them.

Next row: P to last 2 sts, p2tog. *(8 sts)*

Next row: Ssk, k to end. *(7 sts)*

Beg with a p row, work 3 rows in st st.

Next row: Ssk, k3, k2tog. *(5 sts)*

Next row: Purl.

Next row: Ssk, k1, k2tog. *(3 sts)*

Next row: P3tog. *(1 st)*

Break yarn and fasten off.

Transfer 5 sts to second needle and join yarn to rem sts on WS of work.

Next row: Purl.

Next row: Bind (cast) off 2 sts, k2tog, pass 2nd st on right-hand needle over last. *(1 st)*

Break yarn and fasten off.

DELICIOUS EGGS, warm and tasty

2 Make the comb

Using US 3 (3.25mm) needles, cast on 4 sts in red light worsted (DK) yarn. *Bind (cast) off 3 sts, transfer rem st from right-hand to left-hand needle without turning work. Cast on 3 sts.*
Rep from * to * once more.
Bind (cast) off all sts.

3 Make the beak

Using US 3 (3.25mm) needles, cast on 6 sts in yellow light worsted (DK) yarn. Bind (cast) off.

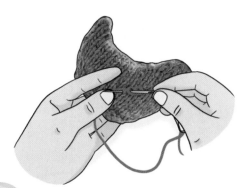

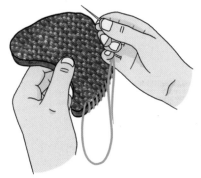

4 Add the embroidered details

Embroider the wings in chain stitch (see page 22) using contrasting yarn. Using black light worsted (DK) yarn, work a French knot for the eye centers (see page 22) and using off-white light worsted (DK) yarn, work a ring of chain stitch around the French knots.

5 Join the pieces

Place the two cozy pieces right sides together. Using the same color yarn as the pieces, oversew (see page 19) around the edges, leaving the base open. Turn the right way out.

6 Add the comb

Oversew the comb in place on top of the head using yarn tails.

7 Add the beak

Fold the beak in half and stitch it in place along this fold using the yarn tails. Weave in all loose ends.

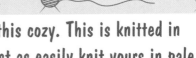

Piglet Hot Water Bottle Cozy

A piglet is the perfect cute animal for this cozy. This is knitted in a lovely piggy-pink yarn, but you could just as easily knit yours in pale gray, white... or any other shade you like.

You will need

Debbie Bliss Rialto Chunky (100% extra-fine merino; 66yd/60m per 1¾oz/50g ball) bulky (chunky) yarn:
  2 balls in shade 031 Blush (pink)

Oddment of black light worsted (DK) yarn

2 x ½in (11mm) dark gray buttons

Black and pink sewing thread

1 x ½in (11mm) snap fastener

US 9 (5.5mm) and US 6 (4mm) knitting needles

Yarn sewing needle

Large-eyed embroidery needle

Standard sewing needle

Gauge (tension)

14 sts and 22 rows in stockinette (stocking) stitch to a 4-in (10-cm) square on US 9 (5.5mm) needles.

Measurements

The finished cozy is 10in (25cm) long when on the hot water bottle and will fit a standard hot water bottle measuring 9½in (24cm) long (including neck) and 6in (15cm) wide.

Abbreviations

k knit
k2tog knit 2 stitches together
m1 make one stitch
p purl
psso pass slipped stitch over
p2tog purl 2 stitches together
purl purlwise
rep repeat
sl slip
ssk slip slip knit
st(s) stitches
st st stockinette (stocking) stitch
* work instructions after or between asterisks (stars) as directed in the pattern

Techniques

Shaping (see pages 14–15)

Sewing up (see page 19)

Sewing on buttons (see page 20)

Embroidery stitches (see page 22)

---

1 **Make the cozy back**
Using US 9 (5.5mm) needles, cast on 24 sts.
Beg with a k row, work 42 rows in st st.
Row 43: K2, k2tog, k to last 4 sts, ssk, k2. *(22 sts)*
Beg with a p row, work 3 rows in st st.*
Rep rows 43–46 (last 4 rows) once more. *(20 sts)*
Bind (cast) off.

2 **Make the cozy front**
Work as for back to *.
Row 47: K2, k2tog, k to last 4 sts, ssk, k2. *(20 sts)*
Row 48: Purl.
Knit 3 rows.
Bind (cast) off.

3 **Make the head (make two)**
Using US 9 (5.5mm) needles, cast on 20 sts.
Beg with a k row, work 2 rows in st st.
Row 3: K2, m1, k to last 2 sts, m1, k2. *(22 sts)*
Row 4: Purl.
Rep rows 3–4 once more. *(24 sts)*

Beg with a k row, work 14 rows in st st.

Row 21: K2, k2tog, k to last 4 sts, ssk, k2. *(22 sts)*

Row 22: Purl.

Row 23: K2, k2tog, k to last 4 sts, ssk, k2. *(20 sts)*

Row 24: P2tog, p to last 2 sts, p2tog. *(18 sts)*

Rep rows 23–24 twice more. *(10 sts)*

Row 29: K2, k2tog, k to last 4 sts, ssk, k2. *(8 sts)*

Row 30: Purl.

Bind (cast) off.

4 **Make the ears (make two)**
Using US 6 (4mm) needles, cast on 7 sts.

Beg with a k row, work 6 rows in st st.

Row 7: K2tog, k3, ssk. *(5 sts)*

Row 8: Purl.

Row 9: K2tog, k1, ssk. *(3 sts)*

Row 10: Sl1 pwise, p2tog, psso. *(1 st)*

Break yarn and fasten off.

SNUGGLE UP...

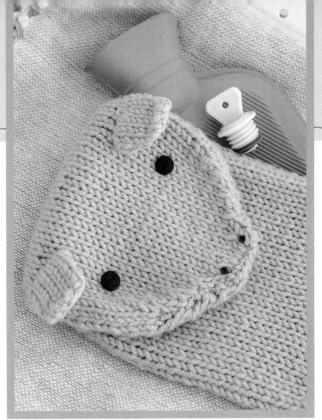

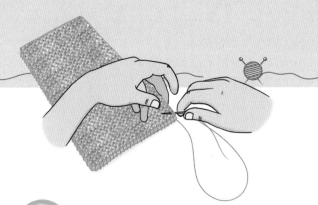

5
Make up the cozy
Oversew the front and back together at the sides and base (see page 19). Sew the two head pieces together in the same way. Oversew the top of the head to the top edge of the back of the body.

6
Add the ears
Oversew (see page 19) the ears in place, using the photograph as a guide.

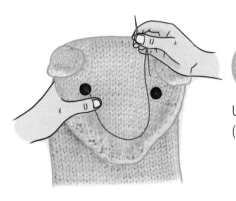

7
Add the eyes and nostrils
For the eyes, sew the buttons in place using black thread (see page 20). Using black yarn, work two French knots (see page 22) for the nostrils.

8
Sew on the snap fastener
Using pink thread, sew one part of the snap fastener in position (see page 20) on the underside of the snout. Fold the flap down and make a tiny pen mark to show where to sew on the other side of the fastener, on the body front. Sew it into position. Weave in all loose ends.

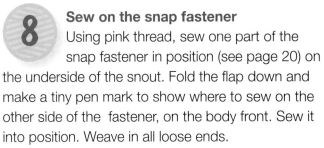

Duck Earphones Cozy

If you're fed up with your earphones getting tangled and tattered, make this cheerful duck cozy. It is knitted using standard light worsted (DK) yarn, but because it is used double, the cozy is thick enough to keep its precious contents really safe.

You will need

Patons Merino Extrafine DK (100% wool; 131yd/120m per 1¾oz/50g ball) light worsted (DK) yarn:
   1 ball in shade 120 Sundance (yellow)

Small amount of light worsted (DK) yarn in a color of your choice for the bow

Small amount of light worsted (DK) yarn in each of deep orange, off-white, and black

US 6 (4mm) and 2/3 (3mm) knitting needles

D-3 (3.25mm) crochet hook or one of a similar size

Yarn sewing needle

Large-eyed embroidery needle

Gauge (tension)

18 sts and 26 rows on stockinette (stocking) stitch to a 4-in (10-cm) square on US 6 (4mm) needles, using yarn doubled.

Measurements

The cozy is 3½in (9cm) in diameter.

Abbreviations

inc increase
k knit
k2tog knit 2 stitches together
m1 make 1
p purl
p2tog purl 2 stitches together
rep repeat
ssk slip slip knit
st(s) stitches
st st stockinette (stocking) stitch
* work instructions after or between asterisks (stars) as directed in the pattern

Techniques

Knitting with two yarns held together (see page 13)

Shaping (see pages 14–15)

Crochet techniques (see page 21)

Sewing up (see page 19)

Embroidery stitches (see page 22)

---

1 **Make the cozy front**
Using US 6 (4mm) needles and yellow yarn doubled, cast on 7 sts.
Row 1: Inc, k to last 2 sts, inc, k1. *(9 sts)*
Row 2: Purl.
Rep rows 1–2 once more. *(11 sts)*
Row 5: K1, m1, k to last st, m1, k1. *(13 sts)*
Row 6: Purl.
Rep rows 5–6 twice more. *(17 sts)*

Beg with a k row, work 4 rows in st st.
*Row 15: K2tog, k to last 2 sts, ssk. *(15 sts)*
Row 16: Purl.
Rep rows 15–16, 3 times more. *(9 sts)*
Row 23: K2tog, k to last 2 sts, ssk. *(7 sts)*
Bind (cast) off pwise.

2 **Make the cozy back (make 2)**
Using US 6 (4mm) needles and yarn doubled, cast on 17 sts in yellow.
Row 1: K1, [p1, k1] to end.
Row 2: P1, [k1, p1] to end.
Beg with a k row, work 2 rows in st st.
Go back to the pattern for the front piece and follow that from * to end.

3 **Make the beak**
Using US 2/3 (3mm) needles and deep orange yarn, cast on 6 sts.
Row 1: Inc, k to last 2 sts, inc, k1. *(8 sts)*
Row 2: Purl.
Row 3: K1, m1, k to last st, m1, k1. *(10 sts)*
Beg with a p row, work 3 rows in st st.
Row 7: K1, k2tog, k4, ssk, k1. *(8 sts)*
Row 8: P2tog, p4, p2tog. *(6 sts)*
Bind (cast) off.

4 **Make the bow**
Using US 2/3 (3mm) needles and chosen yarn, cast on 5 sts.
Row 1: K1, [p1, k1] to end.
Rep row 1, 13 times more.
Bind (cast) off pwise.

5 **Make the head tuft**
Using crochet hook and single strand of yarn, make a 6½-in (17-cm) crochet chain (see page 21).

Tip

If you feel inspired, with a little imagination, you could knit a whole cast of earphone cozy characters; the possibilities are endless.

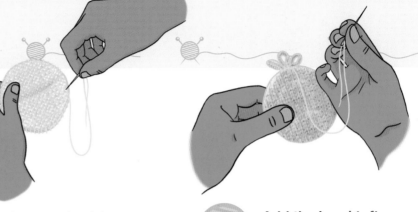

6 **Join the pieces**
Place the back pieces on the front pieces so that the right sides are together and one of the back pieces overlaps the other. Oversew (see page 19) right round the edge. Turn the cozy the right way out and position the right way up, so that the top piece of the back of the head overlaps the bottom piece. The overlap makes the gap where you safely tuck your headphones.

7 **Add the head tuft**
Arrange the crochet chain into three loops and sew in position on top of head.

8 **Make the eyes**
Using black yarn, work French knots (see page 22) for the eye centers. Using off-white yarn, work a circle of chain stitch (see page 22) around each French knot.

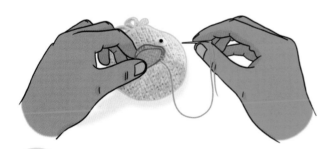

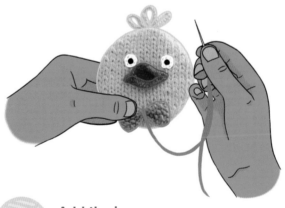

9 **Add the beak**
Fold the beak in half so the cast-on and bound- (cast-) off edges meet and the right side of the piece is on the outside. Sew a few stitches each side of the fold so that it stays in a beak shape, then sew the beak to the cozy along the fold line, with the cast-on edge at the top of the beak.

10 **Add the bow**
Join the bow to the cozy by working a few straight stitches (see page 22) over the center. Weave in all loose ends.

Fluffy Bunny Pillow

This fluffy bunny pillow with its pompom tail is the perfect choice if you want to add a fun touch to a favorite chair. Use different colors to those shown here, if you want it to match your bedroom or another room.

You will need

Rowan Brushed Fleece (65% wool, 30% alpaca, 5% polyester; 114yd/105m per 1¾oz/50g ball) bulky (chunky) yarn:
  2 balls in shade 269 Dawn (pink)
  1 ball in shade 251 Cove (white)

Small amount of fluffy gray yarn (We used Drops Air in shade 04 Medium Grey)

Pillow (cushion) pad measuring 16 x 16in (41 x 41cm)

US 10½ (7mm) knitting needles

Yarn sewing needle

Pompom maker for a 1½-in (4-cm) pompom, or four cardboard circles each measuring 1½in (4cm) in diameter with a ¾-in (2-cm) hole in the center

Gauge (tension)

11½ sts and 16 rows in stockinette (stocking) stitch to a 4-in (10-cm) square on US 10½ (7mm) needles.

Measurements

The cover is for a pillow (cushion) pad measuring 16 x 16in (41 x 41cm). The bunny motif is 5½in (14cm) high.

Abbreviations

k knit
st(s) stitch(es)
st st stockinette (stocking) stitch

Techniques

Using a knitting chart (see step 4, below)

Making pompoms (see page 20)

Sewing up (see page 19)

1 Make the back of the pillow
Cast on 44 sts in the pink yarn.
Beg with a k row, work 62 rows in st st.
Bind (cast) off.

2 Make the front of the pillow
Wind a small ball of pink yarn from the main ball so that you have two balls of pink. Cast on 44 sts using one ball of the pink yarn.
Work 20 rows in st st.

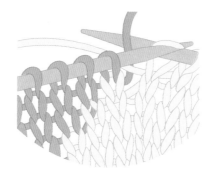

3 Knitting in two colors
Row 21: K17 in pink, and work 1st row of chart (k1 in pink, join in the white yarn and k8 in white, join in the other ball of pink and k1), then k17 in pink. This row sets the position of the stitches shown in the chart. When you change colors, take the strand of the new color up underneath the old one. This twists the strands together and prevents holes appearing. The drawings show how to do this on a knit row (above left), and on a purl row (above right).

4 Knit the rest of the bunny shape from the chart

Work rows 22–42 in st st, completing the bunny motif from the chart (see right), above where you knitted the white stitches on row 21.

Break the white yarn and continue in pink yarn.

Beg with a k row, work 20 rows in st st.

Bind (cast) off.

This knitting chart shows you which stitches to knit in white yarn in order to create the bunny design. Each square represents one stitch and the pattern will tell you when to begin the first row of the chart. The chart is worked from the bottom to the top. On right side rows, follow the chart from right to left. On wrong side rows, follow the chart from left to right. When you've come to the end of the chart, the pattern will tell you what to do next.

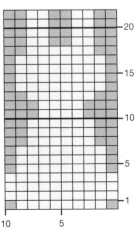

Key

☐ Dawn (pink)
☐ Cove (white)

5 Make the pompom tail
Using the pompom maker or cardboard circles (see page 20), make a pompom in gray yarn. Trim the pompom and use the tails of yarn to sew it in place for the bunny's tail.

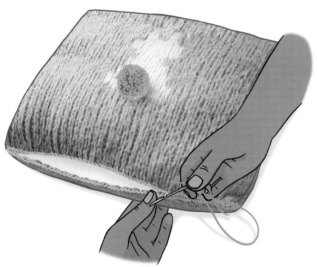

6 Make up the pillow
To make up the pillow, join three of the pillow seams using flat stitch (see page 19), then insert the pad and sew up the final seam. Weave in all loose ends.

Duckling Scarf

Ducks don't mind the rain, so why should you?
Get ready for dull and rainy winter days with this super-cute
fluffy duckling scarf. It's knitted in a combination of wool
and mohair to make sure that it's not just soft and fuzzy,
but is also very warm.

You will need

Rico Soft Merino Aran
(100% merino wool; 109yd/100m
per 1¾oz/50g ball) worsted
(Aran) yarn:
  1 ball in shade 73 Orange

Sugar Bush Yarns Crisp (100%
merino wool; 95yd/87m per
1¾oz/50g ball) light worsted (DK)
yarn:
  2 balls in shade 2024 Juno
  It's Yellow

Rico Essentials Super Kid Mohair
Loves Silk (70% mohair, 30% silk;
219yd/200m per ⅞oz/25g ball)
sport yarn:
  2 balls in shade 017 Yellow

Small amounts of black and
off-white light worsted (DK) yarns

US 9 (5.5mm) knitting needles

Yarn sewing needle

Large-eyed embroidery needle

Gauge (tension)

17 sts and 20 rows in stockinette
(stocking) stitch to a 4-in (10-cm)
square on US 9 (5.5mm) needles
using B and C held together.

Measurements

The finished scarf is 41¼in
(105cm) long.

Abbreviations

inc increase
k knit
k2tog knit 2 stitches together
m1 make 1 stitch
p purl
rem remaining

rep repeat
RS right side
ssk slip slip knit
st(s) stitches
[ ] work the stitches inside the
brackets the number of times it
says after the brackets
* work instructions after or
between asterisks (stars) as
directed in the pattern

Techniques

Shaping (see pages 14–15)

Knitting with two yarns held
together (see page 13)

Embroidery stitches (see page 22)

---

1 **Knit the scarf**
Begin with the
duckling's beak using
the orange yarn and working
from a point to the full width
of the scarf.
Cast on 2 sts in orange.
Row 1: [Inc] twice. *(4 sts)*
Row 2: K1, p2, k1.

Row 3: K1, m1, k to last st, m1,
k1. *(6 sts)*
Row 4: K1, p to last st, k1.
Rep last 2 rows 6 times more.
(18 sts)
Break orange and join in the
two yellow yarns, using the two
yarns held together to knit the
duckling's body.

Row 17: K2, m1, k to last 2 sts,
m1, k2. *(20 sts)*
Row 18: K2, p to last 2 sts, k2.
Rep last 2 rows twice more.
(24 sts)
Row 23: Knit.
Row 24: K2, p to last 2 sts, k2.
Rep rows 23–24, 81 times more.

Now shape the tail which has three long separate feathers.

Row 187: K7 but don't knit the rest of the row. Turn and work on 7 sts you have just knitted only to make one of the long feathers. The other stitches remain on the needle but you don't knit them.

*__Next row:__ K2, p to last 2 sts, k2.
Next row: K3, [k1, p1, k1] all into next st, k3. *(9 sts)*
Next row: K2, p to last 2 sts, k2.
Next row: Ssk, k2, [k1, p1, k1] all into next st, k2, k2tog.
Next row: K2, p to last 2 sts, k2.
Rep last 2 rows, 5 times more.
Next row: K4, [k1, p1, k1] all into next st, k4. *(11 sts)*
Next row: K2, p to last 2 sts, k2.

Next row: K5, [k1, p1, k1] all into next st, k5. *(13 sts)*
Next row: Ssk, p to last 2 sts, k2tog. *(11 sts)*
Next row: Ssk, k to last 2 sts, k2tog. *(9 sts)*
Next row: Ssk, p to last 2 sts, k2tog. *(7 sts)*
Rep last 2 rows once more. *(3 sts)*
Next row: K3tog. *(1 st)*
Break yarn and fasten off.**
Rejoin yarn to rem st you kept on your needle on the RS of work.
Next row: [K1, k2tog] 3 times, k1, turn. Work on 7 sts just knitted only, to make the middle feather of the tail. The other stitches remain on the needle for the last feather but you don't knit them.

Next row: K2, p to last 2 sts, k2.
Next row: K3, [k1, p1, k1] all into next st, k3.
Next row: K2, p to last 2 sts, k2.
Rep from * to ** once more.
Rejoin yarn to rem sts on RS of work.
Next row: Knit.
Rep from * to ** once more.

2 Embroider the eyes

Using black yarn, embroider two coils of chain stitch (see page 22) for the centers of the eyes.

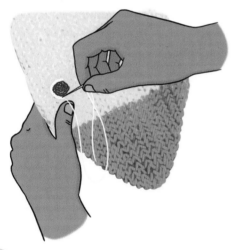

3 Complete the eyes

Work a ring of chain stitch around each eye center using off-white yarn.

4 Add the nostrils

Using black yarn, work two straight stitches (see page 22) on the beak for the nostrils. Weave in all loose ends.

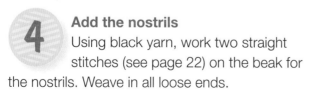

Kitten Bag

This pretty, little kitten bag is double layered to make it strong. This one is knitted in lavender with a soft gray lining, but the yarn comes in lots of fabulous shades. You could choose a color to match a favorite outfit. The bag is finished with a knitted flower—but choose a ready-made bow if you prefer, or leave your kitty plain.

You will need

Cascade Pacific Chunky (60% acrylic, 40% wool; 120yd/110m per 3½oz/100g ball) bulky (chunky) yarn:
  1 ball each in shades:
  38 Violet (lavender)
  15 Taupe (gray)

Small amount of white light worsted (DK) yarn

Very small amounts of black, dark gray, and pink light worsted (DK) yarn

2 x ½-in (12-mm) black buttons

1 x medium-size yellow button

US 10 (6mm), US 9 (5.5mm), and US 6 (4mm) knitting needles

Yarn sewing needle

Large-eyed embroidery needle

Gauge (tension)

12 sts and 14 rows in stockinette (stocking) stitch to a 4-in (10-cm) square on US 10 (6mm) needles.

Measurements

The bag measures 9½in (24cm) across and is 7in (18cm) deep.

Abbreviations

inc increase
k knit
LH left hand
m1 make 1 stitch
p purl
p2tog purl 2 stitches together
RH right hand
ssk slip slip knit
st(s) stitches
st st stockinette (stocking) stitch
WS wrong side

* work instructions after or between asterisks (stars) as directed in the pattern

Techniques

Shaping (see pages 14–15)

Joining in a new color (see page 16)

Sewing up (see page 19)

Sewing on buttons (see page 20)

Embroidery stitches (see page 22)

1 Make the outer bag (make 2)
Using US 10 (6mm) needles, cast on 20 sts in lavender yarn.
Row 1: Inc, k to last 2 sts, inc, k1. *(22 sts)*
Row 2: Purl.
Row 3: K2, m1, k to last 2 sts, m1, k2. *(24 sts)*

Row 4: Purl.
Rep rows 3–4, 4 times more.* *(32 sts)*
Beg with a k row, work 14 rows in st st.
Beg to shape the kitten's two ears.
****Row 27:** K10, bind (cast) off 12 sts, k to end.

Turn and work on the 10 sts you have just knitted to make the first ear. The other stitches remain on the needle but you don't knit them.
Next row: P to last 2 sts, p2tog. *(9 sts)*
Next row: Ssk, k to end. *(8 sts)*
Rep last 2 rows twice more. *(4 sts)*

Next row: [P2tog] twice. *(2 sts)*
Next row: Ssk. *(1 st)*
Fasten off.
To knit the other ear, rejoin yarn
to rem 10 sts on WS of work.
Next row: P2tog, p to end. *(9 sts)*
Next row: K to last 2 sts, k2tog.
(8 sts)
Rep last 2 rows twice more. *(4 sts)*
Next row: [P2tog] twice. *(2 sts)*
Next row: K2tog. *(1 st)*
Fasten off.

2 **Make the bag lining
(make 2)**
Using US 9 (5.5mm)
needles, cast on 20 sts in
gray yarn.
Work as for bag outer to *.
Beg with a k row, work 6 rows
in st st.
Break the gray yarn and join in
the lavender.
Beg with a k row, work 6 rows
in st st.
Work as for bag outer from **
to end.

3 **Make the handle
(make 2)**
Decide how long you
want your handle to be—is
this a shoulder bag or a little
handbag? Using US 10 (6mm)
needles, cast on 5 sts in gray.
Beg with a k row, work
stockinette (stocking) stitch
until the handle is as long as
you want it.
Bind (cast) off. Knit another which
is the same length.

4 Make the flower

Using US 6 (4mm) needles, cast on 10 sts in white yarn.

Row 1: [Inc] twice, turn and work on 4 sts just knitted only.

Beg with a p row, work 11 rows in st st.

Next row: K2tog, ssk, lift RH st over LH st. *(1 st)*

*Next row:** K1 into next cast-on st, inc, turn and work on 4 sts just worked only.

Beg with a p row, work 11 rows in st st.

Next row: K2tog, ssk, lift RH st over LH st. ** *(1 st)*

Rep from * to ** 3 more times.

K into first cast-on st to complete final petal. *(2 sts)*

Bind (cast) off 1 st and fasten off.

5 Make up the bag

With wrong sides together, use flat stitch (see page 19) to sew around the outer lavender pieces from one ear to the other (leaving the top of the bag open). Do the same for the lining pieces but leave a gap in the sewing, big enough to fit your hand into, at the bottom.

6 Add the face

Make a cat face on one of the lavender pieces. Slip a piece of paper or card into the bag to stop you sewing right through to the other side. Sew on the buttons for the eyes using black yarn (see page 20). Pull some of the black yarn apart into separate strands and using one of these work some straight stitches (see page 22) for the eyelashes. Using pink yarn, work a coil of chain stitch (see page 22) for the nose and a line of chain stitch below it. Using dark gray yarn, work some straight stitches for the whiskers.

7 Finish the lining

Turn both the outside bag and the lining inside out. Push the lining inside the main bag so that the pieces are right sides together. Backstitch (see page 19) the main bag and lining together all around the top edge. Turn the bag the right way out through the gap in the base of the lining. Use oversewing (see page 19) to stitch up the hole in the bottom of the lining. Tuck the lining into the main bag.

8 Finish the top edge

Using lavender yarn, oversew around the top edge of the bag to make it strong and neat.

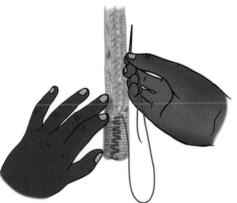

9 Add the handles

Join the long sides of the handle pieces together using flat stitch (see page 19). Secure the handles in place at the top of the bag, using the photograph as a guide.

10 Add the flower

Sew the flower in place and add the yellow button center (see page 20). Weave in all loose ends.

Kitten Scarf

This scarf is knitted in two shades of orange, just like a cute marmalade kitten, but it would look just as beautiful in shades of gray, or even plain black or white. So if you know someone who loves cats, why not knit them this scarf in a shade to match their own pet?

You will need

Patons Merino Extrafine DK (100% wool; 131yd/120m per 1¾oz/50g ball) light worsted (DK) yarn:
   1 ball each in shade 125 Orange
   1 ball each in shade 123 Apricot

Small amounts of black, off-white, and beige light worsted (DK) yarn

US 6 (4mm) knitting needles

Yarn sewing needle

Large-eyed embroidery needle

Gauge (tension)

22 sts and 30 rows in stockinette (stocking) stitch to a 4-in (10-cm) square on US 6 (4mm) needles.

Measurements

The finished scarf is 39¾in (101cm) long, including the back legs.

Abbreviations

inc increase
k knit
k2 tog knit 2 stitches together
k2togtbl knit 2 stitches together through back loop
m1 make 1 stitch
p purl
rem remaining
rep repeat
skpo slip 1 stitch, knit 1 stitch, pass slipped stitch over knitted one, to decrease
st(s) stitch(es)
st st stockinette (stocking) stitch

WS wrong side
[ ] work the stitches inside the brackets the number of times it says after the brackets
* work instructions after or between asterisks (stars) as directed in the pattern

Techniques

Shaping (see pages 14–15)

Carrying yarn up the side of the work (see page 16)

Embroidery stitches (see page 22)

Sewing up (see page 19)

---

1 **Make the scarf**
Cast on 14 sts in orange.
Row 1: Inc, k to last 2 sts, inc, k1. *(16 sts)*
Row 2: Purl.
Row 3: K1, m1, k to last st, m1, k1. *(18 sts)*
Row 4: Purl.
Rep rows 3–4, 5 times more. *(28 sts)*
Beg with a k row, work 17 rows in st st.

Leave orange yarn at side of work and join in apricot.
Row 32: Knit.
Row 33: K2, p to last 2 sts, k2.
Leave apricot at side of work and use orange.
Row 34: Knit.
Row 35: K2, p to last 2 sts, k2.
Rep rows 32–35 (last 4 rows), 53 times more.
Break orange and cont in apricot.
Knit 6 rows.

Now knit the back legs, which are separate with a space between them for the tail.
Row 254: K6, bind (cast) off 16 sts (to make a space for the tail), k to end.
To make the first leg, cont on the 6 stitches you have just knitted only. The remaining stitches, on the other side of the gap, stay on the needle but you don't work them.
Knit 23 rows.

Now shape the paw into toes.

Next row: K2, turn and work on 2 sts just worked only.

*Knit 3 rows.

Next row: K2togtbl, [pick up and k 1 st down row ends, bind (cast) off 1 st] 3 times, k next st on needle, bind (cast) off 1 st, k1. *(2 sts)***

Rep from * to ** once more.

Knit 3 rows.

Next row: K2togtbl, [pick up and k 1 st down row ends, bind (cast) off 1 st] twice.

Break thread and pull rem st through.

Rejoin B to rem 9 sts on WS of work.

Knit 23 rows.

Shape paw as for first back leg.

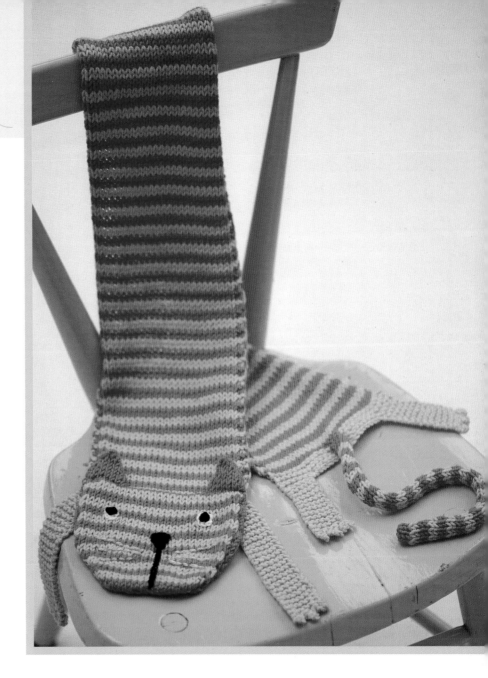

2 **Make the face**
Cast on 14 sts in orange.

Row 1: Inc, k to last 2 sts, inc, k1. *(16 sts)*

Row 2: Purl.

Leave orange at side of work and join in apricot.

Row 3: K1, m1, k to last st, m1, k1. *(18 sts)*

Row 4: Purl.

Leave apricot at side of work and use orange

Row 5: K1, m1, k to last st, m1, k1. *(20 sts)*

Row 6: Purl.

Rep rows 3–6 (last 4 rows) twice more. *(28 sts)*

Leave orange at side of work and use apricot.

Row 15: Knit.

Row 16: Purl.

Leave apricot at side of work and use orange.

Row 17: Knit.

Row 18: Purl.

Rep rows 15–18 (last 4 rows), 3 times more.

Bind (cast) off.

3 Make the front leg (make 2)

Cast on 6 sts in apricot.
Knit 46 rows.
Shape paw as for back legs.

4 Make the ears (make 2)

Cast on 8 sts in orange.
Beg with a k row, work 2 rows in st st.
Row 3: Skpo, k4, k2tog. *(6 sts)*
Row 4: Purl.
Row 5: Skpo, k2, k2tog. *(4 sts)*
Row 6: Purl.

Row 7: Skpo, k2tog. *(2 sts)*
Row 8: P2tog. *(1 st)*
Row 9: Inc. *(2 sts)*
Row 10: Purl.
Row 11: [Inc] twice. *(4 sts)*
Row 12: Purl.
Row 13: K1, m1, k2, m1, k1. *(6 sts)*
Row 14: Purl.

Row 15: K1, m1, k4, m1, k1. *(8 sts)*
Row 16: Purl.
Row 17: Knit.
Bind (cast) off.

5 Make the tail

Cast on 9 sts in orange.
Beg with a k row, work 2 rows in st st.
Leave orange at side of work and join in apricot.
Beg with a k row, work 2 rows in st st.

Rep last 4 rows in two-row stripe pattern like you have just done, 16 times more.
Break apricot and work remainder of tail in orange.
Beg with a k row, work 2 rows in st st.
Next row: Ssk, k5, k2tog. *(7 sts)*

Next row: Purl.
Break yarn, thread it through rem sts, and pull up securely.

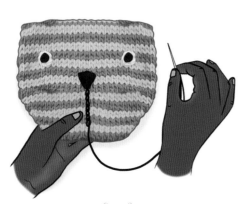

6 Embroider the face

Using black yarn, embroider two small circles using chain stitch (see page 22) for the centers of the eyes. Work a row of chain stitch around these circles using off-white yarn. Using black yarn, work a triangle shape in chain stitch for the nose, then work a line of chain stitch from the base of the nose to the lower edge of the face.

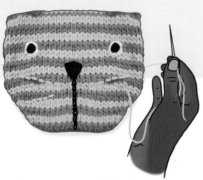

7 Stitch the whiskers
Separate a length of the beige yarn into two thinner strands and use them to embroider the whiskers in backstitch (see page 19).

8 Attach the face
Place the face on the head part of the main scarf so that the right sides are together. Oversew the side seams and lower edge (see page 19). Turn the head the right way out and oversew the top edge in place.

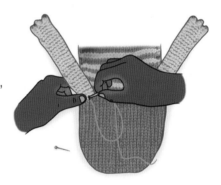

9 Add the legs
Oversew the front legs in place underneath the head, where the head meets the main part of the scarf.

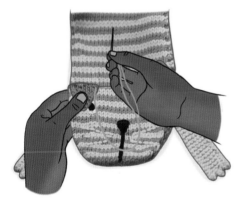

10 Add the ears
Fold the ears so that the right side of the front and back pieces are together and oversew the two sides. Turn the right way out and oversew the lower edge together, then oversew the ears in place using the photograph as a guide.

11 Attach the tail
Fold the two sides of the tail to the back to meet in the middle and sew the seam using flat stitch. Oversew the tail in place in the center of the kitten's lower end, just where the garter stitch border meets the main part of the scarf. Weave in all loose ends.

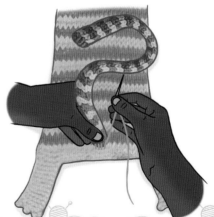

chapter 2

Woodland Creatures

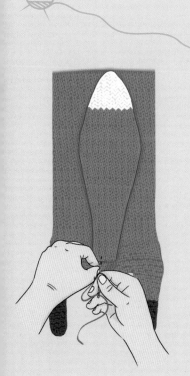

Rabbit Egg Cozies

If you are just getting started on your knitted animal collection, this is a great place to begin. These cute bunny egg cozies will make you smile as they keep your breakfast eggs warm.

You will need

As this is such a small make, you could use any 100%-wool bulky (chunky) yarn to make these. We used:

For the blue cozy
Debbie Bliss Rialto Chunky (100% extra-fine merino; 66yd/60m per 1¾oz/50g ball) bulky (chunky) yarn:
   1 ball in shade 010 Duck Egg (blue)

For the pink cozy
Wendy Merino Chunky (100% merino wool; 71yd/65m per 1¾oz/50g ball) bulky (chunky) yarn:
   1 ball in shade 2473 Rhubarb (pink)

Small amount of off-white bulky (chunky) yarn

Oddment of black light worsted (DK) yarn

US 9 (5.5mm) knitting needles

Yarn sewing needle

Large-eyed embroidery needle

Gauge (tension)

16 sts and 22 rows in stockinette (stocking) stitch to a 4-in (10-cm) square on US 9 (5.5mm) needles on yarns used, but exact gauge is not essential on this project.

Measurements

The cozies are 3½in (9cm) tall and measure 7½in (19cm) around the base.

Abbreviations

k knit
p purl
p2sso pass 2 slipped stitches over
p2tog purl 2 stitches together
rem remaining
sl slip
st(s) stitch(es)
st st stockinette (stocking) stitch
[ ] work the stitches inside the brackets the number of times it says after the brackets

Techniques

Shaping (see pages 14–15)

Sewing up (see page 19)

Embroidery stitches (see page 22)

---

 1 **Make the cozy**
Main piece
   Cast on 32 sts in blue or pink.
Row 1: [K1, p1] to end.
Row 2: [P1, k1] to end.
Row 3: [K1, p1] to end.
Beg with a p row, work 15 rows in st st.
Row 19: K2, [sl2, k1, p2sso, k2] to end. (20 sts)

Row 20: P2tog, p to last 2 sts, p2tog. (18 sts)
Row 21: [Sl2, k1, p2sso] to end. (6 sts)
Break yarn, thread through rem sts, pull firmly, and secure.

2 **Make the ear (make 2)**
   Cast on 4 sts in the same color as the cozy.
Row 1: [K1, p1] twice.
Row 2: [P1, k1] twice.
Rep rows 1–2, 7 times more.
Row 17: P2tog, k2tog. (2 sts)
Row 18: K2tog. (1 st)
Break yarn and fasten off.

3 **Make up the cozy**
Sew the main seam of the cozy using flat stitch (see page 19).

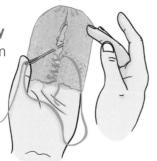

4 **Add the ears**
Fold one ear in half and stitch a couple of stitches through the base to hold the two sides together and give it some shape. Don't cut your thread but use it to sew the ear in place. Do the same for the other ear.

5 **Add the face**
Using black yarn, embroider two small coils of chain stitch (see page 22) for the eyes. Using the same yarn, work a cross stitch (see page 22) for the nose.

6 **Finishing touches**
Using the off-white yarn, work a row of running stitch (see page 22), just above the lower border, using the photograph as a guide. Weave in all loose ends.

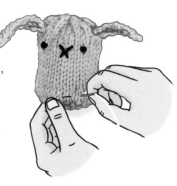

Frog Tissue Case

This cute, goggle-eyed frog tissue case is quick to make, a bit of fun, and makes a lovely gift. You could knit it in soft green, like this, with bright pink girly lips or go for wild whacky tropical colors instead.

You will need

Rowan Pure Wool Superwash DK (100% wool; 137yd/125m per 1¾oz/50g ball) light worsted (DK) yarn:
  1 ball in shade 104 Marl (green)

Small amount of light worsted (DK) yarn in each of pink, off-white, and black

Small amount of fiberfill toy stuffing

US 8 (5mm) and US 3 (3.25mm) knitting needles

Yarn sewing needle

Large-eyed embroidery needle

Gauge (tension)

15 sts and 24 rows in stockinette (stocking) stitch to a 4-in (10-cm) square on US 8 (5mm) needles, using yarn doubled.

Measurements

The finished cozy measures 4¾ x 2¾in (12 x 7cm) and is designed to fit a standard small packet of tissues.

Abbreviations

inc increase
k knit
k2tog knit 2 stitches together
m1 make 1 stitch
p2sso pass 2 slipped stitches over
sl slip
st(s) stitch(es)
st st stockinette (stocking) stitch
[ ] knit the stitches inside the square brackets as many times as the instructions after the brackets tell you

Techniques

Knitting with two yarns held together (see page 13)

Joining in a new color (see page 16)

Shaping (see pages 14–15)

Sewing up (see page 19)

Embroidery stitches (see page 22)

 1 Make the cozy
Using yarn doubled and US 8 (5mm) needles, cast on 20 sts in pink yarn.
Break yarn and join in green, using it doubled.
Beg with a k row, work 32 rows in st st.
Break green and rejoin pink yarn, using it doubled.
Bind (cast) off.

 2 Make the eye hoods (make 2)
Using US 3 (3.25mm) needles and single strand of green, cast on 3 sts.
Row 1: [Inc] 3 times. *(6 sts)*
Row 2: Purl.
Row 3: K1, [m1, k1] to end. *(11 sts)*
Row 4: Knit.
Bind (cast) off.

 3 Make the eyeballs (make 2)
Using US 3 (3.25mm) needles and off-white light worsted (DK) yarn, cast on 4 sts.
Row 1: [Inc] 4 times. *(8 sts)*
Row 2: Purl.
Row 3: K1, [inc] 6 times, k1. *(14 sts)*
Row 4: Purl.
Row 5: [K2tog] to end. *(7 sts)*
Row 6: Purl.
Row 7: K2tog, sl2, k1, p2sso, k2tog. *(3 sts)*
Break yarn, thread it through rem sts, and pull up securely.

4 Sew the mouth seams

With the right side of the cozy facing outward, fold the two short pink edges of the main piece together to form the mouth and oversew (see page 19) the edges of the mouth together 1¼in (3cm) at each side.

5 Sew the side seams

Turn the piece so that the right sides are on the inside and the mouth runs along the horizontal center line. Oversew the two short sides, then turn the piece the right way out.

6 Add the eye hoods

Sew the eye hoods in place so that the bound- (cast-) off edges form the outer rim of the eye hood.

7 Stuff the eyeballs

Join the side seam of the eyeballs using flat stitch (see page 19), stuffing lightly as you go. Place the eyeballs in the eye hoods.

8 Complete the eyes

Stitch in place along the part of the eyeball that meets the top of the main cozy and along the outer rim of the eye hood. Using the black yarn, work a small circle of chain stitch (see page 22) for the eye centers. Weave in all loose ends.

Bug Lip-salve Cozies

Knit up a huge swarm of these cute lip-salve bug cases.
Choose your favorite colors and knit them plain or stripy—
the choice is yours. They are really quick to make, and a great
project for using up leftover yarn.

You will need

For all cozies shown and lots more combinations!

Schachenmayr Catania Fine (100% cotton; 180yd/165m per 1¾oz/50g ball) fingering (4-ply) yarn:
 1 ball each in shades:
 00270 Limone (lime green)
 00100 Schwarz (black)
 00365 Orange (orange)
 00280 Löwenzahn (yellow)
 01002 Tomate (red)

2 x ⅜in (9mm) dark gray buttons for each bug

US 1 (2.25mm) knitting needles

Yarn sewing needle

Large-eyed standard sewing needle

B-1 (2.25mm) crochet hook or one of similar size

Gauge (tension)

35 sts and 40 rows in stockinette (stocking) stitch to a 4-in (10-cm) square on US 1 (2.25mm) needles.

Measurements

The cozies are designed to fit a lip-salve container measuring approx. 2½–2¾in (just under 7cm) long.

Abbreviations

k knit
k2tog knit 2 stitches together
p purl
p2tog purl 2 stitches together
st(s) stich(es)
st st stockinette (stocking) stitch

Techniques

Carrying yarn up the side of the work (see page 16)

Shaping (see pages 14–15)

Sewing up (see page 19)

Sewing on buttons (see page 20)

Crochet techniques (see page 21)

 1 For the lime green and black bug cozy
Body
Cast on 18 sts in lime green yarn.
Beg with a k row, work 6 rows in st st.
Leave lime green yarn at side of work and join in black yarn.
Knit 2 rows.
Leave black at side of work and use lime green.
Beg with a k row, work 4 rows in st st.
Rep last 6 rows three times more.

Cont for another 2 rows in st st using lime green.
Bind (cast) off.

Head
Cast on 22 sts in lime green yarn.
Beg with a k row, work 8 rows in st st.
Row 9: [K2tog] to end. *(11 sts)*
Row 10: P1, [p2tog] to end. *(6 sts)*
Break yarn, thread through rem sts, pull firmly, and secure.

 2 For the orange and yellow bug cozy
Body
Cast on 18 sts in orange yarn.
Beg with a k row, work 32 rows in st st.
Bind (cast) off.

Head
Cast on 22 sts in black yarn.
Break the black yarn and join in the yellow yarn.
Beg with a k row, work 8 rows in st st.

Row 9: [K2tog] to end. *(11 sts)*
Row 10: P1, [p2tog] to end.
(6 sts)
Break yarn, thread through rem sts, pull firmly, and secure.

3 **For the red, lime green, and black bug cozy**

Body
Cast on 18 sts in black yarn.
Beg with a k row, work 7 rows in st st.
Row 8: Knit.
Break the black yarn and join in the red.
Beg with a k row, work 2 rows in st st.
Leave the red at side and join in lime green.

Beg with a k row, work 2 rows in st st.
Keeping to striped pattern, work another 18 rows in st st, so ending with 2 rows in red.
Bind (cast) off.

Head
Cast on 22 sts in red yarn.
Beg with a k row, work 8 rows in st st.
Row 9: [K2tog] to end. *(11 sts)*
Row 10: P1, [p2tog] to end. *(6 sts)*
Break yarn, thread through rem sts, pull firmly, and secure.

4 **Make up the cozy**
Sew the back seam of the body piece using flat stitch (see page 19). Sew the back seam of the head using flat stitch. Sew on button eyes (see page 20).

5 **Add the antennae**
Using a crochet hook and black yarn, make a 1½-in (4-cm) crochet chain (see page 21) for the antennae. Thread the chain in and out of the head part of the bug to form the antennae and trim the yarn close to the chain. Weave in all loose ends.

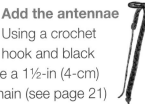

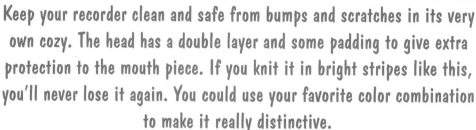

Snake Recorder Case

Keep your recorder clean and safe from bumps and scratches in its very own cozy. The head has a double layer and some padding to give extra protection to the mouth piece. If you knit it in bright stripes like this, you'll never lose it again. You could use your favorite color combination to make it really distinctive.

You will need

Paintbox Yarns Wool Mix Chunky (50% wool, 50% acrylic; 109yd/ 100m per 3½oz/100g ball) bulky (chunky) yarn:
  1 ball each in shades:
  1001 Pure Black
  1022 Buttercup Yellow
  1012 Tomato Red

Small amount of fiberfill toy stuffing

US 10 (6mm) knitting needles

Yarn sewing needle

Large-eyed embroidery needle

F-5 (3.75mm) crochet hook or one of similar size

Gauge (tension)

14 sts and 19 rows in stockinette (stocking) stitch to a 4-in (10-cm) square on US 10 (6mm) needles.

Measurements

The cozy is designed to fit a standard descant recorder approx. 12¾in (32.5cm) long. The finished cozy is 15in (38cm) long excluding the tongue.

Abbreviations

inc increase
k knit
k2tog knit 2 stitches together
p purl
rem remaining
ssk slip slip knit

st(s) stitches
st st stockinette (stocking) stitch
[ ] work the stitches inside the brackets the number of times it says after the brackets
* work instructions after or between asterisks (stars) as directed in the pattern

Techniques

Shaping (see pages 14–15)

Carrying yarn up the side of the work (see page 16)

Crochet techniques (see page 21)

Sewing up (see page 19)

Embroidery stitches (see page 22)

1 **Make the body**
Cast on 7 sts in black yarn.
Row 1: [Inc] to end. *(14 sts)*
Beg with a p row, work 11 rows in st st.
*Leave black at side and join in yellow.
Beg with a k row, work 2 rows in st st.
Leave yellow at side and join in red.
Beg with a k row, work 6 rows in st st.
Leave red at side and join in yellow.
Beg with a k row, work 2 rows in st st.

Leave yellow at side and join in black.
Beg with a k row, work 6 rows in st st.**
Rep from * to ** twice more.
Row 61: [K1, p1] to end.
Rep row 61, 3 times more.
Bind (cast) off keeping to the k1, p1 pattern.

2 **Make the head outer piece**
Cast on 14 sts in black yarn.
Row 1: [K1, p1] to end.
Rep row 1 once more.
Row 3: K2, [m1, k2] to end. *(20 sts)*
Beg with a p row, work 9 rows in st st.
*Row 13: K2, [k2tog] 4 times, [ssk] 4 times,
k2. *(12 sts)*
Row 14: Purl.
Row 15: [K2tog] 3 times, [ssk] 3 times. *(6 sts)*
Break yarn, thread it through rem sts, and pull
up securely.

3 **Make the head inner piece**
Cast on 20 sts in black.
Beg with a k row, work 6 rows in st st.
Work as for head outer piece from * to end.

4 **Make the tongue**
Pull apart a 12-in (30-cm)
length of red yarn and
use three strands only to make
a 3½-in (9-cm) crochet chain
(see page 21).

5 **Make up the body**
Sew the body seam
using flat stitch
(see page 19) and black yarn.

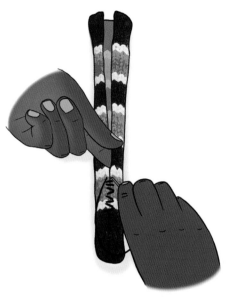

6 Make up the head

Sew up the seam of the outer head piece using flat stitch. Sew up the seam of the inner head piece in the same way. Place a very small handful of toy stuffing in the outer head and spread it up the sides slightly, as if you were lining the piece with it. Turn the inner head piece inside out and push it inside the outer head piece so they are wrong sides together, with the toy stuffing in between to pad them. Oversew (see page 19) the two pieces together from the inside, around the top of the ribbing of the outer head piece.

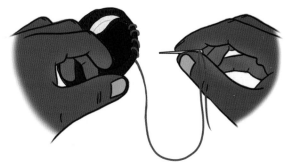

7 Add the face

Separate the strands of a 12-in (30-cm) length of black yarn into two pieces, one with 3 strands and one with 2 strands (the 2-stranded piece can be thrown away). Thread the 3-stranded length onto the needle and work two French knots (see page 22) for the eye centers. Separate a length of yellow yarn in the same way, and work a coil of chain stitch (see page 22) around each eye center, using the photo as a guide.

8 Add the tongue

Fold the crochet chain for the tongue in half and stitch the first ⅜in (1cm) of the folded end together to make a forked tongue. Sew the tongue in place. Weave in all loose ends. If you like, join the head to the body with a loose stitch or two, like a hinge, to make sure the head doesn't go missing.

Rabbit Scarf

This cozy bunny scarf is knitted in a super-bulky yarn, so you'll find it grows really quickly. It's fun making the pompom for the bunny's tail, too.

You will need

Lion Brand Wool-Ease Thick & Quick (80% acrylic, 20% wool; 108yd/98m per 6oz/170g ball) super-bulky (super-chunky) yarn:
  2 balls in shade 105 Glacier (pale blue)
  1 ball in shade 099 Fisherman (white)

Small amounts of black and white light worsted (DK) yarn

US 13 (9mm) knitting needles

Yarn sewing needle

Large-eyed embroidery needle

A pompom maker to make a 4½in (11.5cm) pompom, or two cardboard circles each measuring 4½in (11.5cm) in diameter with a 2¼in (5.5cm) diameter hole in the center

Gauge (tension)

9 sts and 12 rows in stockinette (stocking) stitch to a 4-in (10-cm) square on US 13 (9mm) needles.

Measurements

The finished scarf is 62½in (159cm) long, including the back legs.

Abbreviations

inc increase
k knit
k2tog knit 2 stitches together
p3tog purl 3 stitches together
pwise purlwise
RS right side
ssk slip slip knit
st(s) stitches
st st stockinette (stocking) stitch
WS wrong side
* work instructions after or between asterisks (stars) as directed in the pattern

Techniques

Shaping (see pages 14–15)

Joining in a new color (see page 16)

Embroidery stitches (see page 22)

Sewing up (see page 19)

Making pompoms (see page 20)

1 Make the scarf
Begin with shaping the back of the bunny's head before knitting the straight part of the scarf.
Cast on 12 sts in pale blue.
Row 1: Knit.
Row 2: Purl
Row 3: Inc, k to last 2 sts, inc, k1. *(14 sts)*
Row 4: Purl.
Rep rows 1–4 once more. *(16 sts)*
Row 9: Inc, k to last 2 sts, inc, k1. *(18 sts)*

Row 10: Purl.
Rep rows 9–10 once more. *(20 sts)*
Beg with a k row, work 6 rows in st st.
Row 19: Knit.
Row 20: Knit.
Row 21: K3, p to last 3 sts, k3.
Rep rows 20–21, 75 times more.
Knit 6 rows.
Now shape the back legs so that you have two separate legs hanging down.
Row 177: K5, bind (cast) off 10 sts (to leave a gap between the legs), k to end.

Work on last group of 5 stitches you have just worked. When you reach the gap, turn and don't knit the rest of the row. The other stitches remain on the needle but you don't knit them.
*Knit 7 rows.
Break the pale blue yarn and join in white for the rabbit's paws.
Beg with a k row, work 12 rows in st st.
Shape the paw
Next row: Ssk, k1, k2tog. *(3 sts)*
Next row: P3tog. *(1 st)*

Break yarn and fasten off.**
Rejoin pale blue yarn to second
group of 5 sts on WS of work to
knit the other leg.
Rep from * to ** once.

**Make the front leg
(make 2)**
Cast on 5 sts in
pale blue.
Knit 12 rows.
Break the pale blue yarn and
join in white.
Work 14 rows in st st.
Shape the paw
Row 27: Ssk, k1, k2tog. *(3 sts)*
Break yarn, thread it through rem
sts, and pull up securely.

Make the face
Cast on 12 sts in
pale blue.
Row 1: Knit.
Row 2: Purl
Row 3: Inc, k to last 2 sts, inc,
k1. *(14 sts)*
Row 4: Purl.
Rep rows 1–4 once more.
(16 sts)

Row 9: Inc, k to last 2 sts, inc,
k1. *(18 sts)*
Row 10: Purl.
Rep rows 9–10 once more.
(20 sts)
Beg with a k row, work 6 rows
in st st.
Bind (cast) off.

**Make the ear
(make 2)**
Cast on 4 sts in
pale blue.
Beg with a k row, work 12 rows
in st st.
Row 13: Ssk, k2tog. *(2 sts)*
Row 14: [Inc pwise] twice. *(4 sts)*
Beg with a k row, work 12 rows
in st st.
Bind (cast) off.

5 Embroider the face

Using black yarn, embroider two small circles using chain stitch (see page 22) for the centers of the eyes. Using white yarn, work a circle of chain stitch around the eye centers. For the lashes, use a separated strand of black yarn to work three straight stitches (see page 22) above each eye. Using black yarn, work a cross stitch for the nose (see page 22).

6 Attach the face

Place the face on the head part of the main scarf so that the right sides are together. Oversew the side and lower seams (see page 19). Turn the head the right way out and oversew the top edge in place.

7 Attach the front legs

Oversew the front legs in place underneath the head, where the head meets the main part of the scarf.

8 Add the ears

Fold the ears in half so that the right sides are on the outside and oversew the sides and lower edge. Oversew the ears in place at the top of the head using the photograph as a guide. Using a single stitch, join the back part of the ear to the side of the scarf, to make the ears stand up.

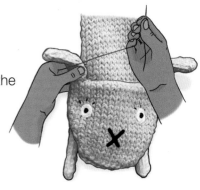

9 Make the tail

Make a white pompom, using the pompom maker or cardboard circles (see page 20) and white yarn. When you finish off the pompom by winding yarn around the center and knotting it, leave one end of the yarn long. Thread a needle onto this end and use it to sew the pompom in place just above the garter stitch border at the lower end of the scarf. Weave in all loose ends.

Hanging Birds

These birds are quick to knit, so you can easily make a flock of them. As they don't use much yarn, it is a good project to use up any leftovers. This chain of birds would look great hanging in a corner of your bedroom or make one in pastel colors for a new baby in the family.

You will need

Cascade Cherub DK (55% nylon, 45% acrylic; 180yd/165m per 1¾oz/50g ball) light worsted (DK) yarn:
  1 ball each in shades:
  13 Jade (green)
  15 Orchid (pink)
  28 Boy Blue (blue)
  17 Grey (gray) (for the cord and tassel)

Very small amounts of black and yellow light worsted (DK) yarns

A few handfuls of fiberfill toy stuffing

US 3 (3.25mm) knitting needles

US D-3 (3.25mm) crochet hook or one of similar size

Yarn sewing needle

Large-eyed embroidery needle

Gauge (tension)

25 sts and 34 rows in stockinette (stocking) stitch to a 4-in (10-cm) square on US 3 (3.25mm) needles.

Abbreviations

inc increase
k knit
k2tog knit 2 stitches together
m1 make 1 stitch

p purl
p2tog purl 2 stitches together
pwise purlwise
ssk slip slip knit
st(s) stitch(es)
st st stockinette (stocking) stitch
* work instructions after or between asterisks (stars) as directed in the pattern

Techniques

Shaping (see pages 14–15)

Crochet techniques (see page 21)

Sewing up (see page 19)

Embroidery stitches (see page 22)

---

1 **Make the birds**
First side
Cast on 15 sts.
Row 1: Inc, k to last 2 sts, inc, k1. *(17 sts)*
Row 2: Purl.
Row 3: K1, m1, k to last st, m1, k1. *(19 sts)*
Row 4: Purl.
Rep rows 3–4, 3 times more.* *(25 sts)*
Beg with a k row, work 6 rows in st st.

Row 17: Bind (cast) off 14 sts, k to end. *(11 sts)*
Beg with a p row, work 5 rows in st st.
**Row 23: K1, k2tog, k to last 3 sts, ssk, k1. *(9 sts)*
Row 24: P2tog, p5, p2tog. *(7 sts)*
Row 25: K1, k2tog, k1, ssk, k1. *(5 sts)*
Bind (cast) off pwise.

Second side
Work as for first side to *.
Beg with a k row, work 5 rows in st st.
Row 16: Bind (cast) off 14 sts pwise, p to end. *(11 sts)*
Beg with a k row, work 6 rows in st st.
Work as for first side from ** to end.

Repeat to make two more birds in the other yarn colors.

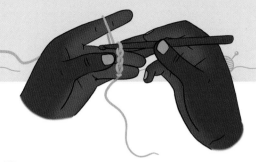

2 Make the hanging cords

Using the crochet hook and gray yarn, make four lengths of crochet chain (see page 21), one 8-in (20-cm) long chain for the top and three 3-in (8-cm) long chains. Leave tails of yarn at the start and end of each chain for sewing onto the birds.

3 Make the tassel

Wrap gray yarn around four fingers approximately 20 times. Ease the yarn off your fingers and thread the tail of one of the short crochet chains you have just made through the loops. Tie it tightly around them to hold them together, knotting it just where the crochet begins so the tassel hangs just below the crochet. Tie a short length of gray yarn around the tassel about ½in (1cm) down from the top, tying it as tightly as possible—this is easier with someone to help you. To finish the tassel, cut through the loops and trim them so that they are all the same length.

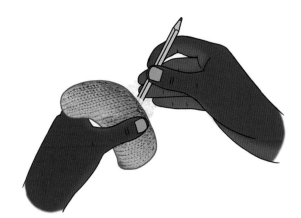

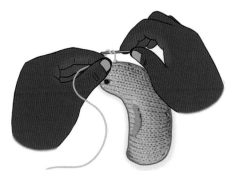

4 Make up the birds

Place the two pieces for each bird right sides together. Oversew (see page 19) around the outer edge, leaving the lower edge open for turning and stuffing. Turn the piece right sides out. Stuff fairly lightly and close the lower edge using flat stitch (see page 19).

5 Embroider the details

Using the yarn double, embroider the wings in chain stitch (see page 22) using the photograph as a guide. Using black yarn, work French knots (see page 22) for the eyes. Using yellow yarn, work French knots for the beaks.

6 Join up the birds

Join the birds together with the lengths of crochet chain, sewing the tails of yarn at the ends of the chains to the tops and bottoms of the birds. Make sure the long length is attached to the top bird and the tassel is at the bottom. Form the free end of the top length into a loop for hanging. Weave in all loose ends.

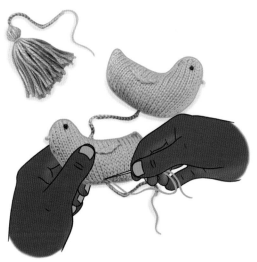

Come FLY WITH ME

Raccoon Tablet Cozy

Tablets are very useful but expensive gadgets, so keep yours safe by knitting this cozy to protect it from bumps and scratches. Check whether your tablet is the same size as the one here before you begin.

You will need

James C Brett Chunky with Merino (70% acrylic, 20% polyamide, 10% merino; 164yd/150m per 3½oz/100g ball) bulky (chunky) yarn:
  1 ball each in shades:
  09 (gray)
  03 (white)

Sirdar Country Style DK (40% nylon, 30% wool, 30% acrylic; 170yd/155m per 1¾oz/50g ball) light worsted (DK) yarn:
  1 ball in shade 417 Black

1 x ¾in (22mm) black button

1 x ½in (11mm) snap fastener

US 9 (5.5mm) knitting needles

Yarn sewing needle

Large-eyed embroidery needle

Gauge (tension)

15 sts and 21 rows in stockinette (stocking) stitch to a 4-in (10-cm) square on US 9 (5.5mm) needles.

Measurements

The cozy is designed to fit a tablet measuring approx. 9½ x 7¼in (24 x 18.5cm). For tablets of other sizes you would need to adjust the pattern. You may know an expert knitter who could help you do this.

Abbreviations

inc increase
k knit
k2tog knit 2 stitches together
kwise knitwise
m1 make 1 stitch
p purl
p2tog purl 2 stitches together

pwise purlwise
rem remaining
ssk slip slip knit
st(s) stitches
st st stockinette (stocking) stitch
* work instructions after or between asterisks (stars) as directed in the pattern

Techniques

Joining in a new color (see page 16)

Shaping (see pages 14–15)

Knitting with two yarns held together (see page 13)

Embroidery stitches (see page 22)

Sewing up (see page 19)

Sewing on buttons (see page 20)

1 **Make the front of the cozy**
Cast on 28 sts in gray.
Beg with a k row, work 46 rows in st st.
Knit 4 rows.
Bind (cast) off.

2 **Make the back of the cozy**
Cast on 28 sts in gray.
Beg with a k row, work 48 rows in st st.
Bind (cast) off.

3 **Make the face**
First wind a couple of yards/meters of black yarn around your hand and cut it from the main ball to make a second ball.
Now cast on 28 sts in gray.
Beg with a k row, work 4 rows in st st.

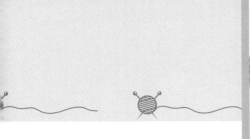

Break the gray yarn and join in the white.

Row 5: K2, k2tog, k to last 4 sts, ssk, k2. *(26 sts)*

Row 6: Purl.

Rep rows 5–6 once more. *(24 sts)*

Break the white yarn and join in the black, taking the yarn from both balls to make a double strand.

Row 9: K2, k2tog, k to last 4 sts, ssk, k2. *(22 sts)*

Row 10: Purl.

Rep rows 9–10 twice more. *(18 sts)*

Break black and join in white.

***Row 15:** K2, k2tog, k to last 4 sts, ssk, k2. *(16 sts)*

Row 16: Purl.

Rep rows 15–16, 4 times more. *(8 sts)*

Row 25: K2, k2tog, ssk, k2. *(6 sts)*

Row 26: P2tog, p2, p2tog. *(4 sts)*

Row 27: Ssk, k2tog. *(2 sts)*

Break yarn, thread it through rem sts, and secure.

 Make the underside of the head

Cast on 28 sts in gray. Beg with a k row, work 4 rows in st st.

Row 5: K2, k2tog, k to last 4 sts, ssk, k2. *(26 sts)*

Row 6: Purl.

Rep rows 5–6, 4 times more. *(18 sts)*

Break gray and join in white.

Cont as for face from * to end.

 Make the ears (make 2)

Cast on 6 sts in gray. Beg with a k row, work 4 rows in st st.

Row 5: Ssk, k2, k2tog. *(4 sts)*

Row 6: [P2tog] twice. *(2 sts)*

Row 7: K2tog. *(1 st)*

Row 8: Inc pwise. *(2 sts)*

Row 9: [Inc] twice. *(4 sts)*

Row 10: Purl.

Row 11: K1, m1, k2, m1, k1. *(6 sts)*

Beg with a p row, work 4 rows in st st.

Bind (cast) off kwise.

PROTECT your tech

6 Add the eyes
On the black stripe across the raccoon's face, embroider the eyes in chain stitch (see page 22) using white yarn.

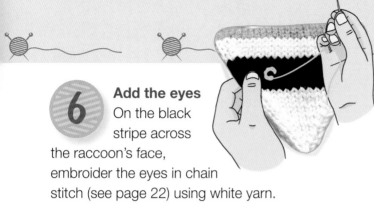

7 Join the head pieces
Place the face and head underside pieces right sides together and oversew (see page 19) the sides. Turn the head the right way out and oversew the top edges (see page 19).

8 Add the ears
Fold the ear pieces so the right sides are together and oversew along the two sides, leaving the lower edges open for turning. Turn the right way out, oversew along lower edge, and oversew the ears in position.

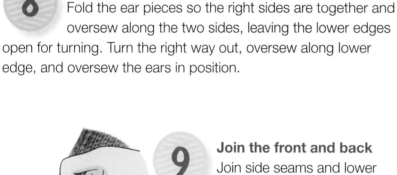

9 Join the front and back
Join side seams and lower edges of main cozy in flat stitch.

10 Attach the head
Oversew top of head to top edge of back of main cozy. Sew the button in place for the nose (see page 20).

11 Add the fastener
Sew the top of the snap fastener under the button (see page 20). Fold the flap down and make a tiny pen mark to show where to sew on the other side of the fastener, on the body front. Sew it into position. Weave in all loose ends.

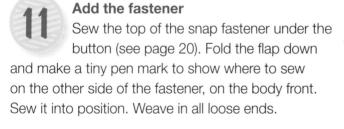

Owl Storage Baskets

Knit yourself some handy storage baskets for keeping all your bits and pieces tidy—they are great for items such as pencils, hair elastics, and tiny toys. They are knitted in seed (moss stitch) which is very easy and gives them a lovely texture.

You will need

Debbie Bliss Roma (70% wool, 30% alpaca; 87yd/80m per 3½oz/100g ball) super-bulky (super-chunky) yarn:
  1 ball in shade 008 Citrus (yellow)

Small amounts of dark gray and orange light worsted (DK) yarns

A very small amount of off-white light worsted (DK) yarn

2 x ½-in (12-mm) pale blue buttons for larger basket

2 x ⁵⁄₁₆-in (8-mm) pale blue buttons for smaller basket

Black sewing thread

A very small amount of fiberfill toy stuffing

US 15 (10mm) and US 7 (4.5mm) knitting needles

Yarn sewing needle

Large-eyed embroidery needle

Standard sewing needle

Gauge (tension)

10 sts and 13 rows in stockinette (stocking) stitch to a 4-in (10-cm) square on US 15 (10mm) needles.

Measurements

The finished larger basket stands 6½in (16.5cm) tall and the smaller one 3½ in (9cm) tall.

Abbreviations

k knit
k2tog knit 2 stitches together
p purl
psso pass slipped stitch over
p2tog purl 2 stitches together
rem remaining
sl slip
ssk slip slip knit
st(s) stitch(es)
st st stockinette (stocking) stitch
[ ] work the stitches inside the brackets the number of times it says after the brackets

Techniques

Shaping (see pages 14–15)

Knitting with two yarns held together (see page 13)

Sewing up (see page 19)

Sewing on buttons (see page 20)

For the large owl

Make the large basket
Using US 15 (10mm) needles, cast on 34 sts.
Beg with a k row, work 4 rows in st st.
Row 5: [K1, p1] to end.
Row 6: [P1, k1] to end.
Rep rows 5–6, 12 times more.
Row 31: [K2tog] to end. *(17 sts)*
Row 32: Knit.
Row 33: K1, [k2tog] to end. *(9 sts)*
Row 34: Knit.
Break yarn and thread through rem sts.

Make the wings for the large basket (make 2)
Using US 15 (10mm) needles, cast on 5 sts.
Row 1: [K1, p1] to last st, k1.
Rep row 1, 5 times more.
Row 7: P2tog, k1, p2tog. *(3 sts)*
Row 8: P1, k1, p1.
Row 9: Sl1, k2tog, psso. *(1 st)*
Fasten off.

Make the eye bases for the large basket (make 2)
Using dark gray yarn double and US 7 (4.5mm) needles, cast on 20 sts.
Row 1: [K2tog] to end. *(10 sts)*
Row 2: [P2tog] to end. *(5 sts)*
Break yarn, leaving a long strand. Thread a yarn sewing needle with this strand of yarn, then take it through rem sts and slip them off the needle. Pull the yarn tight to close up the sts. Put the two short edges right sides together and oversew (see page 19) them together.

Make the beak for the large basket
Using orange yarn double and US 7 (4.5mm) needles, cast on 8 sts.
Beg with a k row, work 2 rows in st st.
Row 3: K1, ssk, k2, k2tog, k1. *(6 sts)*
Row 4: P2tog, p2, p2tog. *(4 sts)*
Break yarn and thread through rem sts, and secure.

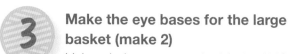

Always **TIDY** as you go!

For the small owl

5 **Make the small basket**
Using US 15 (10mm) needles, cast on 22 sts.
Beg with a k row, work 4 rows in st st.
Row 5: [K1, p1] to end.
Row 6: [P1, k1] to end.
Rep rows 5–6, 5 times more.
Row 17: [K2tog] to end. *(11 sts)*
Row 18: Knit.
Row 19: K1, [k2tog] to end. *(6 sts)*
Row 20: Knit.
Break yarn and thread through rem sts.

6 **Make the wings for the small basket (make 2)**
Using US 15 (10mm) needles, cast on 3 sts.

7 **Make the eye bases for the small basket (make 2)**
Using dark gray yarn double and US 7 (4.5mm) needles, cast on 16 sts.
Row 1: [K2tog] to end. *(8 sts)*
Row 2: [P2tog] to end. *(4 sts)*
Break yarn, leaving a long strand.

Row 1: K1, p1, k1.
Rep row 1, 4 times more.
Row 6: Sl1, k2tog, psso. *(1 st)*
Fasten off.

Thread a yarn sewing needle with this strand of yarn, then take it through rem sts and slip them off the needle. Pull the yarn tight to close up the sts. Put the two short edges right sides together and oversew (see page 19) them together.

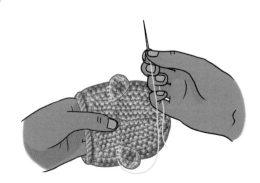

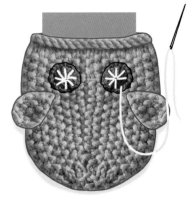

8 **Make the beak for the small basket**
Using orange yarn double and US 7 (4.5mm) needles, cast on 6 sts.
Beg with a k row, work 2 rows in st st.
Row 3: K1, ssk, k2tog, k1. *(4 sts)*
Break yarn and thread through rem sts, and secure.

9 **Make up the basket (both sizes are the same)**
Join the lower and back seam of the basket using flat stitch (see page 19). Oversew (see page 19) the wings in position at the sides.

10 **Add the eyes**
Oversew the eye bases in position.
Using off-white yarn and straight stitch (see page 22), work 8-point stars on the eye bases of the larger basket and 6-point stars on the eye bases of the smaller basket, using the photograph as a guide.

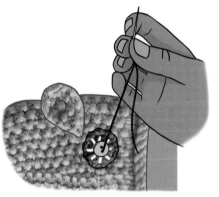

Add the buttons
Sew the buttons
(see page 20) in
place using black thread.

Add the beak
Sew the long seam
of the beak, leaving
the lower edge open. Push a
tiny amount of stuffing into
the beak to make it stand
out and oversew the beak in
place. Weave in all loose ends.

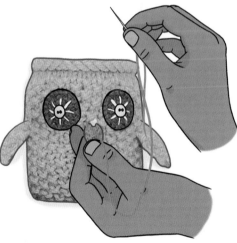

Fox Scarf

Wear this friendly fox scarf around your neck and let him dangle. Or wind him so his face and front legs are at the front and his back legs and lovely bushy tail hang down the back. There are a lot of different pieces to make, but none take very long and the result is a very striking scarf.

You will need

Katia Peru (40% wool, 40% acrylic, 20% alpaca; 115yd/106m per 3½oz/100g ball) bulky (chunky) yarn:
   3 balls in shade 16 (orange)
   1 ball in shade 2 (black)

Bergere de France Merinos Alpaga (60% merino, 40% alpaca; 71yd/65m per 1¾oz/50g ball) bulky (chunky) yarn:
   1 ball in shade 29899 Ecru (white)

Small amounts of black and off-white light worsted (DK) yarn

US 10 (6mm) knitting needles

Yarn sewing needle

Large-eyed embroidery needle

Gauge (tension)

14 sts and 18 rows in stockinette (stocking) stitch to a 4-in (10-cm) square on US 10 (6mm) needles using the orange yarn.

Measurements

The finished scarf is approximately 54in (137cm) long, including the back legs.

Abbreviations

inc increase
k knit
k2tog knit 2 stitches together
kwise knitwise
m1 make 1 stitch
p purl
p2tog purl 2 stitches together
psso pass slipped stitch over
purl purlwise

rem remaining
sl slip
ssk slip slip knit
st st stockinette (stocking) stitch
st(s) stitch(es)
WS wrong side
[ ] work the stitches inside the brackets the number of times it says after the brackets
* work instructions after or between asterisks (stars) as directed in the pattern

Techniques

Shaping (see pages 14–15))

Joining in a new color (see page 16)

Embroidery stitches (see page 22)

Sewing up (see page 19)

---

1 **Make the scarf beginning with the back of the pointed face.**
Cast on 2 sts in orange yarn.
Row 1: [Inc] twice. *(4 sts)*
Row 2: Purl.
Row 3: K1, m1, k2, m1, k1. *(6 sts)*
Row 4: Purl.
Row 5: K1, m1, k to last st, m1, k1. *(8 sts)*
Row 6: Purl.
Rep rows 5–6, 8 times more. *(24 sts)*
Beg with a k row, work 7 rows in st st.
Row 30: Knit.

Row 31: K3, p to last 3 sts, k3.
Rep rows 30–31, 95 times more.
Rows 222-227: Knit.
Now knit the back legs which are separate with a space between them for the tail.
Row 228: K7, bind (cast) off 10 sts (to make a space for the tail), k to end.
Turn and work the group of 7 stitches you have just knitted only. The remaining stitches, on the other side of the gap, stay on the needle but you don't work them.*Knit 11 rows.

Break the orange yarn and join in black yarn to make the black paw.
Knit 16 rows.

Shape paw

Next row: K1, k2tog, k1, ssk, k1. *(5 sts)*

Next row: K2tog, k1, ssk. *(3 sts)*

Next row: Sl1, k2tog, psso. *(1 st)*
Break yarn and fasten off.
Now knit the other back paw using the 7sts you left on the needle so with WS of main body facing, rejoin the orange yarn to remaining 7 sts.
Work from * to end.

2 **Make the front leg (make 2)**
Using orange yarn, cast on 7 sts.
Knit 26 rows.
Break the orange yarn and work remainder of leg in black to make the black paw.
Knit 24 rows.

Shape the paw

Next row: K1, k2tog, k1, ssk, k1. *(5 sts)*

Next row: K2tog, k1, ssk. *(3 sts)*

Next row: Sl1, k2tog, psso. *(1 st)*
Break yarn and fasten off.

3 **Make the face**
Cast on 2 sts in orange yarn.

Row 1: [Inc] twice. *(4 sts)*

Row 2: Purl.

Row 3: K1, m1, k2, m1, k1. *(6 sts)*

Row 4: Purl.

Row 5: K1, m1, k to last st, m1, k1. *(8 sts)*

Row 6: Purl.
Rep rows 5–6, 8 times more. *(24 sts)*
Beg with a k row, work 7 rows in st st.
Bind (cast) off.

4 Make the ears (make 2)

Cast on 12 sts in orange yarn.
Beg with a k row, work 2 rows in st st.
Row 3: K1, ssk, k6, k2tog, k1. *(10 sts)*
Row 4: Purl.
Row 5: K1, ssk, k4, k2tog, k1. *(8 sts)*
Row 6: Purl.
Row 7: K1, ssk, k2, k2tog, k1. *(6 sts)*
Row 8: Purl.
Row 9: K1, ssk, k2tog, k1. *(4 sts)*
Row 10: [P2tog] twice. *(2 sts)*
Row 11: K2tog. *(1 st)*
Row 12: Inc pwise. *(2 sts)*
Row 13: [Inc] twice. *(4 sts)*
Row 14: Purl.
Row 15: K1, m1, k2, m1, k1. *(6 sts)*
Row 16: Purl.
Row 17: K1, m1, k4, m1, k1. *(8 sts)*
Row 18: Purl.
Row 19: K1, m1, k6, m1, k1. *(10 sts)*
Row 20: Purl.
Row 21: K1, m1, k8, m1, k1. *(12 sts)*
Beg with a p row, work 2 rows in st st.
Bind (cast) off kwise.

5 Make the tail

Cast on 8 sts in orange yarn.
Row 1: Inc, k to last 2 sts, inc, k1. *(10 sts)*
Beg with a p row, work 3 rows in st st.
Row 5: K2, m1, k to last 2 sts, m1, k2. *(12 sts)*
Beg with a p row, work 3 rows in st st.
Row 9: K3, m1, k to last 3 sts, m1, k3. *(14 sts)*
Beg with a p row, work 3 rows in st st.
Row 13: K4, m1, k to last 4 sts, m1, k4. *(16 sts)*
Beg with a p row, work 3 rows in st st.
Rep last 4 rows once more. *(18 sts)*
Row 21: K5, m1, k to last 5 sts, m1, k5. *(20 sts)*
Beg with a p row, work 3 rows in st st.
Rep last 4 rows once more. *(22 sts)*
Row 29: K6, m1, k to last 6 sts, m1, k6. *(24 sts)*
Beg with a p row, work 3 rows in st st.
Rep last 4 rows once more. *(26 sts)*
Beg with a k row, work 6 rows in st st.
Row 43: K6, ssk, k10, k2tog, k6. *(24 sts)*
Beg with a p row, work 3 rows in st st.
Row 47: K5, ssk, k10, k2tog, k5. *(22 sts)*

Beg with a p row, work 3 rows in st st.

Row 51: K5, ssk, k8, k2tog, k5. *(20 sts)*

Row 52: Purl.

Break the orange yarn and join in the white yarn to make the tip of the tail.

Row 53: Knit.

Row 54: Purl.

Row 55: K4, ssk, k8, k2tog, k4. *(18 sts)*

Beg with a p row, work 3 rows in st st.

Row 59: K4, ssk, k6, k2tog, k4. *(16 sts)*

Row 60: Purl.

Row 61: K3, ssk, k6, k2tog, k3. *(14 sts)*

Row 62: Purl.

Row 63: K3, ssk, k4, k2tog, k3. *(12 sts)*

Row 64: Purl.

Row 65: K2, ssk, k4, k2tog, k2. *(10 sts)*

Row 66: Purl.

Row 67: K1, [ssk] twice, [k2tog] twice, k1. *(6 sts)*

Row 68: P2tog, p2, p2tog. *(4 sts)* Break yarn, thread it through rem sts, and pull up securely.

6 **Embroider the eyes**
On the face, using black light worsted (DK) yarn, work two small coils of black chain stitch (see page 22) for the centers of the eyes. Using off-white light worsted (DK) yarn, work a circle of chain stitch around the eye centers.

7 **Embroider the nose and lashes**
Using black light worsted (DK) yarn, work a coil of chain stitch for the nose. Using the same yarn, work three straight stitches (see page 22) above each eye for the lashes.

8 **Add the head**
Place the face on the head part of the main scarf so that the right sides are together. Oversew the side seams (see page 19). Turn the head the right way out and sew the top edge in place using flat stitch (see page 19).

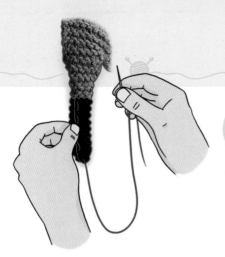

9 Sew up the back legs

Sew the seam of the black part of the back legs using flat stitch. Continue ¾in (2cm) into the orange part of the leg

10 Add the front legs

As in step 9, sew the sides of the black part of the front legs together using flat stitch, continuing 2in (5cm) into the orange part of the leg. Oversew the front legs in place underneath the head, where the head meets the main part of the scarf.

11 Add the ears

Fold the ears so that the right side of the front and back pieces are together and oversew the two sides. Turn the right way out and oversew the lower edges. Oversew the ears in place.

12 Add the tail

Sew the back seam of the tail using flat stitch and matching yarns. Oversew the tail in place in the center of the fox's lower end, just where the garter stitch border meets the main part of the scarf. Weave in all loose ends.

Mouse Tea Cozy

This cute mouse tea cozy will brighten up your breakfast table and keep your tea good and hot! This cozy is a beautiful pale gray with just a hint of pink, but you can make your mouse dark gray, black, white, or brown—or any fantasy mouse color you love.

You will need

Debbie Bliss Cashmerino Aran (55% wool, 33% acrylic, 12% cashmere; 98yd/90m per 1¾oz/50g ball) worsted (Aran) yarn:
   1 ball in shade 027 Stone (gray)

Small amount of pale pink light worsted (DK) yarn

2 x ⅜in (8mm) black dome buttons

A handful of fiberfill toy stuffing

Black sewing thread

US 7 (4.5mm) knitting needles

Yarn sewing needle

Standard sewing needle

Gauge (tension)

20 sts and 27 rows in stockinette (stocking) stitch to a 4-in (10-cm) square on US 7 (4.5mm) needles, using gray yarn.

Measurements

The cozy will fit a 2-cup teapot that is 4.5in (11cm) tall. The actual cozy is 4¼in (10.5cm) tall and has a circumference of 9½in (24cm).

Abbreviations

inc increase
k knit
k2tog knit 2 stitches together
m1 make 1 stitch
p2sso pass 2 slipped stitches over
p2tog purl 2 stitches together
pwise purlwise
rem remaining
sl slip
ssk slip slip knit
st(s) stitch(es)
st st stockinette (stocking) stitch
[ ] work the stitches inside the brackets the number of times it says after the brackets

Techniques

Shaping (see pages 14–15)

Sewing up (see page 19)

Sewing on buttons (see page 20)

Embroidery stitches (see page 22)

1 Make the cozy (make 2)

Cast on 24 sts in gray yarn.
Row 1: Knit.
Beg with a k row, work 4 rows in st st.
Row 6: K2, [m1, k4] 5 times, m1, k2. *(30 sts)*
Beg with a p row, work 21 rows in st st.

Row 28: K1, [sl2, k1, p2sso, k2] 5 times, sl2, k1, p2sso, k1. *(18 sts)*
Row 29: Purl.
Row 30: [Sl2, k1, p2sso] to end. *(6 sts)*
Break yarn, thread through rem sts, pull firmly, and secure.

2 Make the head

Cast on 34 sts in gray yarn.

Beg with a k row, work 2 rows in st st.

Row 3: K6, ssk, k1, k2tog, k12, ssk, k1, k2tog, k6. *(30 sts)*

Row 4: Purl.

Row 5: K5, ssk, k1, k2tog, k10, ssk, k1, k2tog, k5. *(26 sts)*

Row 6: Purl.

Row 7: K4, ssk, k1, k2tog, k8, ssk, k1, k2tog, k4. *(22 sts)*

Row 8: Purl.

Row 9: K3, ssk, k1, k2tog, k6, ssk, k1, k2tog, k3. *(18 sts)*

Row 10: Purl.

Row 11: K2, ssk, k1, k2tog, k4, ssk, k1, k2tog, k2. *(14 sts)*

Row 12: Purl.

Row 13: K1, ssk, k1, k2tog, k2, ssk, k1, k2tog, k1. *(10 sts)*

Row 14: Purl.

Row 15: Ssk, k1, k2tog, ssk, k1, k2tog. *(6 sts)*

Break yarn, thread through rem sts, pull firmly, and secure.

3 Make the ears (make 2)

Cast on 3 sts in A.

Row 1: [Inc] 3 times. *(6 sts)*

Beg with a p row, work 3 rows in st st.

Row 5: K1, ssk, k2tog, k1. *(4 sts)*

Row 6: [P2tog] twice. *(2 sts)*

Row 7: [Inc] twice. *(4 sts)*

Row 8: [Inc pwise, p1] twice. *(6 sts)*

Beg with a k row, work 3 rows in st st.

Row 12: [P2tog] 3 times. *(3 sts)*

Bind (cast) off.

4 Make the tail

Cast on 5 sts in pink yarn.

Beg with a k row, work 60 rows in st st.

Row 61: Ssk, k1, k2tog. *(3 sts)*

Break yarn, thread through rem sts, pull firmly, and secure.

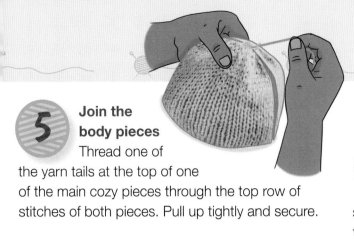

5 Join the body pieces
Thread one of the yarn tails at the top of one of the main cozy pieces through the top row of stitches of both pieces. Pull up tightly and secure.

6 Sew the sides
Sew down 2½in (6cm) at the top of both sides with flat stitch (see page 19) and sew up ½in (1.5cm) at the bottom of both sides, so that you leave a space for the handle and spout.

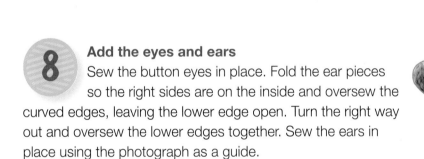

7 Attach the head
Sew the seam of the head using flat stitch to make a cone shape and push some stuffing into it. With the seam at the bottom, oversew (see page 19) the head in position. If you need to, push in a little more stuffing to make the head firm before you finish the stitching.

8 Add the eyes and ears
Sew the button eyes in place. Fold the ear pieces so the right sides are on the inside and oversew the curved edges, leaving the lower edge open. Turn the right way out and oversew the lower edges together. Sew the ears in place using the photograph as a guide.

9 Add the nose
Using pink yarn, work a spiral of chain stitches (see page 22) around the point of the head to make the nose.

10 Add the tail
With wrong sides together, oversew the long seam of the tail and then stitch in place. Weave in all loose ends.

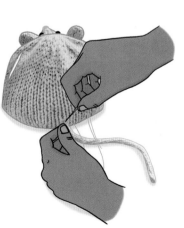

chapter 3
Wildlife

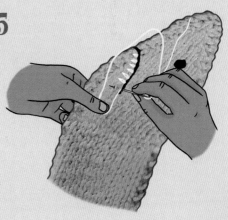

Zebra Cowl

If you're a newbie knitter, or just fancy working on something quick, this is the perfect project for you. The yarn is really chunky, so the knitting will grow at a cracking pace.

You will need

Lion Brand Wool-Ease Thick & Quick (82% acrylic, 10% wool, 8% rayon; 108yd/98m per 6oz/170g ball) super-bulky (super-chunky) yarn:
  1 ball each in shades:
  153 Black
  099 Fisherman (white)

US 13 (9mm) knitting needles

Yarn sewing needle

Gauge (tension)

9 sts and 12 rows in stockinette (stocking) stitch to a 4-in (10-cm) square on US 13 (9mm) needles.

Measurements

The finished cowl measures 26½in (67cm) in circumference and is 12½in (32cm) deep.

Abbreviations

k knit
st st stockinette (stocking) stitch
st(s) stitch(es)

Techniques

Carrying yarn up the side of the work (see page 16)

Sewing up (see page 19)

Make the cowl
Cast on 60 sts in black.
Beg with a k row, work 2 rows in st st.
Leave black yarn at side of work and join in white yarn.
Beg with a k row, work 2 rows in st st.
Leave white at side of work and use black.
Beg with a k row, work 2 rows in st st.
Rep rows 2–6 (last 4 rows), 8 times more.
Bind (cast) off.

Sew up the seam
To make up the cowl, sew the back seam of cowl using flat stitch (see page 19).

Finishing off
Weave in all the loose ends.

Super-stylish **STRIPES**

Tiger Phone Cozy

This stripy cozy is the perfect way to protect your phone. It has a flap that tucks in the back so when your phone is snuggled inside, it will stay safe and secure.

You will need

Lion Brand Wool-Ease (80% acrylic, 20% wool; 196yd/180m per 3oz/85g ball) worsted (Aran) yarn:
  1 ball each in shades:
  171 Gold
  153 Black

Small amount of light worsted (DK) yarn in off-white

US 6 (4mm) and US 3 (3.25mm) knitting needles

Yarn sewing needle

Large-eyed embroidery needle

Gauge (tension)

19 sts and 25 rows in stockinette (stocking) stitch to a 4-in (10-cm) square on US 6 (4mm) needles.

Measurements

The cozy will be a fairly snug fit on a phone that measures just under 5½in by just over 2½in (14 x 7cm). The finished cozy measures 6 x 3¼in (15 x 8cm) unstretched. If your phone is bigger than this, you can add a few stitches to the width or a few extra rows to the length of the cozy.

Abbreviations

k knit
k2tog knit 2 stitches together
p purl
ssk slip slip knit
st(s) stitch(es)
st st stockinette (stocking) stitch

Techniques

Carrying yarn up the side of the work (see page 16)

Shaping (see pages 14–15)

Sewing up (see page 19)

Embroidery stitches (see page 22)

 1 Make the back
Using US 6 (4mm) needles, cast on 18 sts in gold yarn.
Row 1: [K1, p1] to end.
Rep row 1, 3 times more.
Rows 5–8: Beg with a k row, work 4 rows in st st.
Leave the gold yarn at side and join in black.
Rows 9–10: Beg with a k row, work 2 rows in st st.
Leave black at side and pick up gold.

Rows 11–14: Beg with a k row, work 4 rows in st st.
Leave gold at side and pick up black.
Rows 15–16: Beg with a k row, work 2 rows in st st.
Rep rows 11–16 (last 6 rows) twice more.
Break black, cont in gold.
Beg with a k row, work 8 rows in st st.
Bind (cast) off.

 2 Make the front
Using US 6 (4mm) needles, cast on 18 sts in gold yarn.
Row 1: Knit.
Row 2: K2, p to last 2 sts, k2.
Rep rows 1–2, 4 times more.
Rows 15–24: Beg with a k row, work 14 rows in st st.
Leave gold at side and join in black.
Rows 25–26: Beg with a k row, work 2 rows in st st.

Leave black at side and pick up gold.

Rows 27–30: Beg with a k row, work 4 rows in st st.

Leave gold at side and pick up black.

Rows 31–32: Beg with a k row, work 2 rows in st st.

Rep rows 27–32 (last 6 rows) once more.

Break black, cont in gold.

Beg with a k row, work 8 rows in st st.

Bind (cast) off.

 Make the ears (make 2)

Using US 3 (3.25mm) needles, cast on 5 sts in gold yarn.

Knit 3 rows.

Row 4: Ssk, k1, k2tog. *(3 sts)*

Row 5: K3tog. *(1 st)*

Fasten off.

Tip

When knitting the stripes, you don't have to break the yarn at the end of each stripe. You can just take it up the side of your work, catching it in over your needle from time to time as you begin a new row so that you don't get big loops of yarn at the side—see also page 16.

Perfect PROTECTOR

Sew the seams

4 Sew the side and bottom seams using flat stitch (see page 19), matching the stripes. Remember that the first 10 rows of the front, where you have worked the garter stitch border, form a flap to tuck in at the back.

Add the ears

5 Oversew (see page 19) the ears in place.

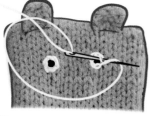

Add the eyes

6 Using black yarn, make two French knots (see page 22) for the eye centers. Using the off-white yarn, work a circle of chain stitch (see page 22) around each French knot.

Add the nose

7 Using black yarn, add the nose using straight stitches (see page 22), using the photograph as a guide. Weave in all loose ends.

Rattlesnake Scarf

This is one of the easier animal scarves to knit. The two-color pattern is also very easy to do, and you can feel free to choose any two colors you think work brilliantly together.

You will need

Katia Peru (40% wool, 40% acrylic, 20% alpaca; 116yd/106m per 3½oz/100g ball) bulky (chunky) yarn:
   1 ball in shade 028 (purple)

King Cole Magnum Chunky (70% acrylic, 30% wool; 120yd/110m per 3½ oz/100g ball) bulky (chunky) yarn:
   1 ball in shade 1441 Steel (gray)

Small amount of bulky (chunky) yarn in cream

Small amounts of black and coral light worsted (DK) yarn

Small handful of fiberfill toy stuffing

US 10½ (6.5mm) needles

J/10 (6mm) crochet hook or one of similar size

Yarn sewing needle

Large-eyed embroidery needle

Gauge (tension)

14 sts and 18 rows in stockinette (stocking) stitch to a 4-in (10-cm) square on US 10½ (6.5mm) needles for both yarns.

Measurements

The finished scarf is approximately 65in (165cm) long, including the knotted tail.

Abbreviations

inc increase
k knit
k2tog knit 2 stitches together
m1 make 1 stitch
p purl
psso pass slipped stitch over
rem remaining

rep repeat
ssk slip slip knit
sl1 slip 1 stitch
st(s) stitch(es)
[ ] work the stitches inside the brackets the number of times it says after the brackets

Techniques

Shaping (see pages 14–15)

Carrying yarn up the side of the work (see page 16)

Knitting in two colors (see page 17)

Crochet techniques (see page 21)

Sewing up (see page 19)

Embroidery stitches (see page 22)

1 **Make the scarf**
Begin by shaping the head.
Cast on 7 sts in purple.
Row 1: Inc, k to last 2 sts, inc, k1. *(9 sts)*
Row 2: Knit.
Row 3: Inc, k to last 2 sts, inc, k1. *(11 sts)*
Row 4: K2, p to last 2 sts, k2.
Row 5: K1, m1, k to last st, m1, k1. *(13 sts)*

Row 6: K2, p to last 2 sts, k2.
Rep last 2 rows, 4 times more. *(21 sts)*
Row 15: Knit.
Row 16: K2, p to last 2 sts, k2.
Rep rows 15–16, 3 times more. Leave the purple yarn at side of work and join in the gray yarn. This is where you begin the two-color pattern.
Row 23: Knit 2 stitches in gray, then knit 1 stitch in purple,

followed by 1 stitch in gray and keep going 1 stitch purple, 1 stitch gray, until you reach the last 3 stitches, then knit 1 stitch in purple and 2 in gray.
Row 24: In gray, k2, p to last 2 sts, k2.
Row 25: In gray, knit the whole row.
Row 26: Knit 2 stitches in gray, then purl 1 in purple followed by 1 in gray and keep going in purl,

rattlesnake scarf 93

1 stitch purple, 1 stitch gray, until the last 3 stitches, then purl 1 in purple and knit 2 in gray.

Row 27: In purple, knit whole row.

Row 28: In purple, k2, p to last 2 sts, k2.

Rep rows 23–28, 36 times more.
Rep rows 23–24 once more.
Break purple and work remainder of scarf in gray. This is where you begin to shape the tail.

Row 247: K2, ssk, k to last 4 sts, k2tog, k2. *(19 sts)*

Row 248: K2, p to last 2 sts, k2.

Row 249: Knit.

Row 250: Purl.

Rep rows 247–250, 5 times more. *(9 sts)*

Row 271: K2, ssk, k1, k2tog, k2. *(7 sts)*

Row 272: K2, p to last 2 sts, k2.

Row 273: Knit.

Row 274: K2, p to last 2 sts, k2.

Row 275: K1, ssk, k1, k2tog, k1. *(5 sts)*

Knit 25 rows.

Row 301: Ssk, k1, k2tog. *(3 sts)*

Row 302: Sl1, k2tog, psso. *(1 st)*
Break yarn and fasten off.

2 **Make the eye hoods (make 2)**
Cast on 3 sts in purple.

Row 1: [Inc] twice, k1. *(5 sts)*

Row 2: Knit.

Row 3: K1, [m1, k1] to end. *(9 sts)*

Row 4: Knit.
Bind (cast) off.

3 **Make the eyeballs (make 2)**
Cast on 3 sts in cream.

Row 1: [Inc] 3 times. *(6 sts)*

Row 2: Purl.

Row 3: K1, [m1, k1] to end. *(11 sts)*

Row 4: Purl.

Row 5: [K2tog] twice, sl1, k2tog, psso, [ssk] twice. *(5 sts)*
Break yarn, thread it through rem sts, and pull up securely.

Not-so SCARY snake!

4 Make the tongue

Using the crochet hook and the coral light worsted (DK) yarn double, work a 5-in (13-cm) crochet chain (see page 21).

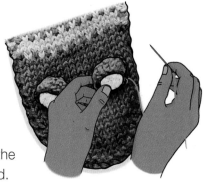

5 Complete the eyes

Sew the eye hoods in place so that the bound- (cast-) off edges form the outer rim of the eye hood. Join the side seam of the eyeballs using flat stitch (see page 19), stuffing lightly as you go. Place the eyeballs in the eye hoods and stitch in place along the part of the eyeball that meets the main scarf and along the outer rim of the eye hood.

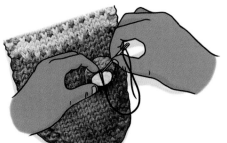

6 Embroider the eyes

Using black light worsted (DK) yarn, work 3 long straight stitches (see page 22) close together for the eye centers.

7 Attach the tongue

Thread the crochet chain for the tongue through the tip of the head and match the two ends. Sew the first ¾in (2cm) of the strands, nearest to the head, together to form the forked end.

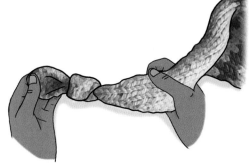

8 Finish the tail

Make a knot in the end of the tail. Weave in all loose ends.

Panda Mug Hug

Everyone loves a panda and now you can create your own cuddly mug-hugging versions for both a standard-size cup and something a bit more giant, just like the creature itself. Not only do these mug hugs look great, they'll help keep your favorite drinks warm, too.

You will need

Wendy Mode Chunky (50% wool, 50% acrylic; 153yd/140m per 3½oz/100g ball) bulky (chunky) yarn:
  1 ball each in shade:
  202 Vanilla (white)
  220 Coal (black)

Small amounts of bright colored bulky (chunky) yarns for the collars and bows

1 x ¾in (18mm) gray button for each cozy

US 8 (5mm) knitting needles

Yarn sewing needle

Large-eyed embroidery needle

Stitch markers or small safety pins

White sewing thread

Gauge (tension)

16 sts and 22 rows in stockinette (stocking) stitch to a 4-in (10-cm) square on US 8 (5mm) needles.

Measurements

The smaller cozy fits a standard ½ pint (300ml) and the larger cozy fits a 1 pint (600ml) mug. The smaller cozy is 3¼in (8.5cm) deep and has a 9½in (24cm) circumference. The larger cozy is 4¼in (10.5cm) deep and has an 11½in (29cm) circumference. Figures for the larger cozy are given in brackets after the figures for the smaller cozy. Measure the mug you want to use the cozy on and decide which one to make.

Abbreviations

inc increase
k knit
k2tog knit 2 stitches together
kwise knitwise
p purl
p2tog purl 2 stitches together
pwise purlwise
RH right hand
RS right side
ssk slip slip knit
st(s) stitch(es)
st st stockinette (stocking) stitch

Techniques

Joining in a new color
(see page 16)

Picking up stitches (see page 18)

Shaping (see pages 14–15)

Sewing up (see page 19)

Embroidery stitches (see page 22)

Sewing on buttons (see page 20)

---

1 **Make the main part of the mug hug**
Cast on 38 (46) sts using a bright colored yarn for the collar.
Knit 2 rows.
Break collar yarn and join in white.
Beg with a p row, work 16 (20) rows in st st, noting instructions below.

For smaller size, mark beginning and end of 5th and 12th rows on RH side with stitch markers, safety pins, or contrasting thread.

For larger size, mark beginning and end of 6th and 15th rows on RH side with stitch markers, safety pins, or contrasting thread.
Bind (cast) off kwise.

2 **Make the tab**
For the smaller cozy, with RS facing pick up and knit 6 sts evenly between 5th and 12th rows, checking that the tab knitted here will fit neatly through your mug handle and adjusting the position if necessary.
Row 2: K2, p2, k2.
Row 3: Knit.
Row 4: K2, p2, k2.
Rep rows 3–4 twice more.
Row 9: K2, bind (cast) off 2 sts, k to end. *(4 sts)*
Row 10: K2, turn and cast on 2 sts, turn back and k to end. *(6 sts)*
Row 11: Knit.
Row 12: Bind (cast) off tightly.

For the larger cozy, with RS facing pick up and knit 8 sts evenly between 6th and 15th row, checking that the tab knitted from here will fit centrally through the mug handle and adjusting the position if necessary.
Row 2: K2, p4, k2.
Row 3: Knit.
Row 4: K2, p4, k2.
Rep rows 3–4 twice more.
Row 9: K3, bind (cast) off 2 sts, k to end. *(6 sts)*
Row 10: K3, turn and cast on 2 sts, turn back and k to end. *(8 sts)*
Row 11: Knit.
Row 12: Bind (cast) off tightly.

3 **Make the ears (make 2)**
Cast on 6 sts in black yarn.
Beg with a k row, work 4 rows in st st.
Row 5: K2tog, k2, ssk. *(4 sts)*
Row 6: [P2tog] twice. *(2 sts)*
Row 7: [Inc] twice. *(4 sts)*
Row 8: [Inc pwise, p1] twice. *(6 sts)*
Beg with a k row, work 4 rows in st st.
Bind (cast) off.

4. Make the eye patches (make 2)

Cast on 2 sts in black yarn.
Row 1: [Inc] twice. *(4 sts)*
Beg with a p row, work 3 rows in st st.
Row 5: K2tog, ssk. *(2 sts)*
Row 6: P2tog. *(1 st)*
Fasten off.

5. Make the bow

Cast on 22 sts in the same color yarn as you used for the collar.
Bind (cast) off.

6. Make up the ears

Fold the ear pieces in half, right sides together and oversew (see page 19) around the curved edges, leaving the flat edge open for turning. Turn the ears the right way out and oversew together at the base. Oversew in position.

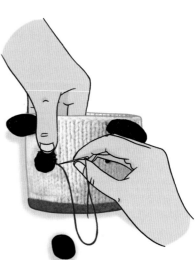

7. Add the eye patches

Oversew the eye patches in position using the photograph as a guide.

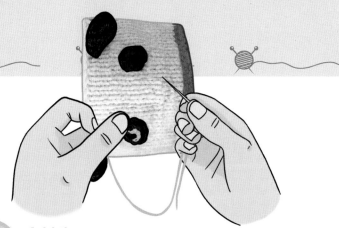

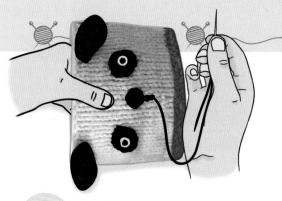

8 **Add the eyes**
Pull apart a 12in (30cm) length of black yarn into two thinner strands. Use these to work a French knot (see page 22) for the eye centers in the middle of each eye patch, making sure you can see its position on the black eye patch. Pull apart a length of white yarn in the same way and work a circle of chain stitch (see page 22) around the eye centers.

9 **Add the nose**
Using a separated length of black, work a coil of chain stitches for the nose and add a line of chain stitches underneath, using the photograph as a guide.

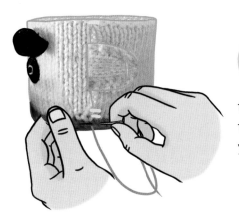

10 **Join the seams**
Join the top and bottom edges of the side seams using flat stitch (see page 19), leaving a gap in the middle the size of your mug handle. Use white yarn for the white parts but finish off with a few stitches of colored yarn to join the collar.

11 **Add the bow and button**
Stitch the two short ends of the bow piece together to make a loop but don't cut the yarn. Instead, with the seam in the middle at the back, make the loop into a bow and secure it in place on the front of the collar by stitching over and over the center point. Fit the mug cozy over the mug, with the tab through the handle and mark the center of the buttonhole. Sew the button (see page 20) where the mark is. Weave in all loose ends.

Shark Scarf

Sharks can appear scary, but not this one: this is certainly the most adorable shark you'll ever meet. This lovely fellow is cool-looking and sleek, but warm and cozy too, and utterly irresistible.

You will need

Red Heart Lisa Big (100% acrylic; 131yd/120m per 7oz/200g ball) super-bulky (super-chunky) yarn:
  1 ball in shade 00198 Grey

Small amounts of black, white, and dark gray light worsted (DK) yarn

US 13 (9mm) knitting needles

2 x stitch markers or small safety pins

Yarn sewing needle

Large-eyed embroidery needle

Gauge (tension)

9 sts and 13 rows in stockinette (stocking) stitch to a 4-in (10-cm) square on US 13 (9mm) needles.

Measurements

Scarf is 41in (104cm) long.

Abbreviations

inc increase
k knit
k2tog knit 2 stitches together
m1 make 1 stitch
p purl
psso pass slipped stitch over
rep repeat
RS right side

skpo slip 1, knit 1, pass slipped stitch over (1 stitch decrease)
sl1 slip 1 stitch
ssk slip slip knit
st(s) stitch(es)
WS wrong side
[ ] work the stitches inside the brackets the number of times it says after the brackets

Techniques

Shaping (see pages 14–15)

Embroidery stitches (see page 22)

---

1 **Scarf**
Begin by shaping the head.

Cast on 2 sts in gray.
Row 1: Inc, k1. *(3 sts)*
Row 2: Knit.
Row 3: [Inc] twice, k1. *(5 sts)*
Row 4: K2, p1, k2.
Row 5: K2, m1, k to last 2 sts, m1, k2. *(7 sts)*
Row 6: K2, p to last 2 sts, k2.
Row 7: Knit.
Row 8: K2, p to last 2 sts, k2.
Rep rows 5–8, 4 times more. *(15 sts)*
Row 25: Knit.

Row 26: K2, p to last 2 sts, k2.
Rep rows 25–26, 12 times more.
Row 51: Knit.
With RS facing, mark left-hand end of row with a stitch marker or small safety pin.
Row 52: P to last 2 sts, k2.
Rep rows 51–52, 7 times more.
Row 67: Knit.
With RS facing, mark left-hand end of row with a stitch marker or small safety pin.
Row 68: K2, p to last 2 sts, k2.
Rep rows 67–68, 7 times more.
Row 83: K2, ssk, k to last 4 sts, k2tog, k2. *(13 sts)*

Row 84: K2, p to last 2 sts, k2.
Row 85: Knit.
Row 86: K2, p to last 2 sts, k2.
Rep rows 85–86, 4 times more.
Rep rows 83–94 (last 12 rows) once more. *(11 sts)*
Row 107: K2, ssk, k to last 4 sts, k2tog, k2. *(9 sts)*
Row 108: K2, p to last 2 sts, k2.
Row 109: Knit.
Row 110: K2, p to last 2 sts, k2.
Rep rows 109–110 twice more.
Now shape the tail which has two separate fins.
Row 115: K2, m1, k to last 2 sts, m1, k2. *(11 sts)*

Row 116: K2, p to last 2 sts, k2. Rep rows 115–116 three times more. *(17 sts)*

Row 123: K2, m1, k6, but don't knit the rest of the row. Turn and work on the 10 stitches you have just knitted to make the first fin. The other stitches remain on the needle but you don't knit them.

Next row: K2, p to last 2 sts, k2.

Next row: Knit to last 4 sts, k2tog, k2. *(8 sts)*

Next row: K2, p to last 2 sts, k2. Rep last 2 rows, 3 times more. *(5 sts)*

Next row: K1, k2tog, k2. *(4 sts)*

Next row: Knit.

Next row: K2tog, k2. *(3 sts)*

Next row: Sl1, k2tog, psso. *(1 st)* Break yarn and fasten off. Now knit the other fin. Rejoin yarn to rem 9 sts still on the needle on RS of work.

Next row: Knit to last 2 sts, m1, k2. *(10 sts)*

Next row: K2, p to last 2 sts, k2.

Next row: K2, skpo, k to end. *(9 sts)*

Next row: K2, p to last 2 sts, k2. Rep last 2 rows, 4 times more. *(5 sts)*

Next row: K2, skpo, k1. *(4 sts)*

Next row: Knit.

Next row: K2, skpo. *(3 sts)*

Next row: Sl1, skpo, pass first slipped stitch over. Break yarn and fasten off.

2 Make the dorsal fin

The dorsal fin is knitted onto the part of the edge without the garter stitch border. With RS facing, pick up and k 15 sts across center edge of scarf, between the two stitch markers.

Row 1 (WS): K1, p to last st, k1.
Row 2: K1, m1, k to last 3 sts, skpo, k1.
Row 3: K1, p2tog, p to last st, k1. *(14 sts)*
Rep rows 2–3, 3 times more. *(11 sts)*
Row 10: Knit to last 3 sts, skpo, k1. *(10 sts)*
Row 11: K1, p2tog, p to last st, k1. *(9 sts)*
Rep rows 10–11 twice more. *(5 sts)*
Row 16: K2tog, k1, skpo. *(3 sts)*
Row 17: Sl1, k2tog, psso. *(1 st)*
Break yarn and fasten off.

3 Embroider the face

Using black yarn, embroider a small coil of chain stitch (see page 22) for the eye and a line of chain stitch for the mouth. Using white yarn, embroider some chain stitches for the teeth.

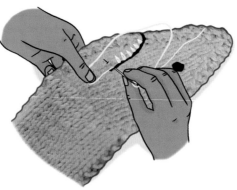

4 Add the gills

Using dark gray yarn, work three curved lines of chain stitch for the gills. Weave in all loose ends.

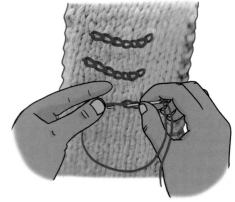

Elephant Hot Water Bottle Cozy

This brilliant elephant hot water bottle cozy will keep you feeling snug and cheerful on chilly winter nights. It's knitted in a gorgeous bluish-gray yarn—a true elephant color— but light and dark grays, or even pink, would look cute.

You will need

Rowan Cocoon (80% merino wool, 20% mohair; 126yd/115m per 3¾oz/100g ball) bulky (chunky) yarn:
  1 ball in shade 836 Moon (gray)

Small amount of off-white bulky (chunky) yarn

2 x ½in (11mm) dark gray buttons

Black sewing thread

1 x ½in (11mm) snap fastener

US 9 (5.5mm) and US 7 (4.5mm) knitting needles

Yarn sewing needle

Standard sewing needle

Gauge (tension)

13 sts and 19 rows in stockinette (stocking) stitch to a 4-in (10-cm) square on US 9 (5.5mm) needles.

Measurements

The finished cozy is 10in (25cm) long when on the hot water bottle and will fit a standard hot water bottle measuring 9½in (24cm) long (including neck) and 6in (15cm) wide.

Abbreviations

k knit
k2tog knit 2 stitches together
p purl
p2tog purl 2 stitches together
ssk slip slip knit
st(s) stitches
st st stockinette (stocking) stitch
[ ] knit the stitches inside the square brackets as many times as the instructions after the brackets tell you

Techniques

Shaping (see pages 14–15)

Sewing up (see page 19)

Sewing on buttons (see page 20)

1 — Make the back of the cozy

Using US 9 (5.5mm) needles, cast on 22 sts in gray yarn.

Beg with a k row, work 42 rows in st st.

Bind (cast) off.

2 — Make the front of the cozy

Using US 9 (5.5mm) needles, cast on 22 sts in gray yarn.

Beg with a k row, work 40 rows in st st.

Knit 2 rows.

Bind (cast) off.

3 — Make the head and trunk (make 2)

Using US 9 (5.5mm) needles, cast on 22 sts in gray yarn.

Beg with a k row, work 20 rows in st st.

Row 21: K2, ssk, k to last 4 sts, k2tog, k2. *(20 sts)*

Row 22: P2tog, p to last 2 sts, p2tog. *(18 sts)*

Row 23: Bind (cast) off 4 sts, k to end. *(14 sts)*

Row 24: Bind (cast) off 4 sts pwise, p to end. *(10 sts)*

Row 25: Ssk, k to last 2 sts, k2tog. *(8 sts)*

Row 26: Purl.

Rep rows 25–26 once more. *(6 sts)*

Beg with a k row, work 10 rows in st st.

Bind (cast) off.

4 Make the ears (make 2)

Using US 9 (5.5mm) needles, cast on 20 sts in gray yarn.

Beg with a p row, work 3 rows in st st.

Row 4: [K2tog] to end. *(10 sts)*

Row 5: P2tog, p to last 2 sts, p2tog. *(8 sts)*

Row 6: [Ssk] twice, [p2tog] twice. *(4 sts)*

Row 7: [K2tog] twice. *(2 sts)*

Row 8: P2tog. *(1 st)*

Break yarn and fasten off.

5 Make the tusks (make 2)

Using US 7 (4.5mm) needles, cast on 4 sts in off-white.

Beg with a k row, work 4 rows in st st.

Row 5: Ssk, k2tog. *(2 sts)*

Row 6: P2tog. *(1 st)*

Break yarn and fasten off.

6 Join the pieces

Sew the front and back together at the sides and base using flat stitch (see page 19). Sew around the head pieces in the same way, leaving the short end of the trunk unstitched. Oversew the top of the head to the top edge of the back of the body.

7 Add the ears

Oversew (see page 19) the ears in place using the photograph as a guide.

8 Add the eyes and tusks

Sew on the buttons (see page 20) for the eyes. Oversew the edges of the tusks together, then stitch the tusks in place.

9 Add the snap fastener

Sew one part of the snap fastener in position (see page 20) on the underside of the trunk between the tusks. Close the flap and mark where the other side of the snap fastener needs to be on the front of the cozy. Sew it in place. Weave in all loose ends.

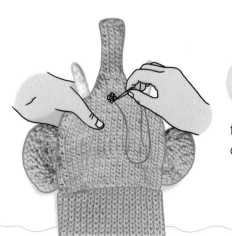

Bear Hat

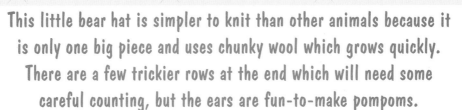

This little bear hat is simpler to knit than other animals because it is only one big piece and uses chunky wool which grows quickly. There are a few trickier rows at the end which will need some careful counting, but the ears are fun-to-make pompoms.

You will need

Plymouth Yarn Encore Chunky (75% acrylic, 25% wool; 142yd/130m per 3½oz/100g ball) bulky (chunky) yarn:
   1 ball in shade 240 Grey

Oddment of light worsted (DK) yarn in black

2 x ½in (12mm) shiny black shank buttons

US 9 (5.5mm) knitting needles

Pompom maker to make 1¾in (4.5cm) pompoms, or four cardboard circles each measuring 1¾in (4.5cm) in diameter with a ¾in (18mm) hole in the center

Yarn sewing needle

Large-eyed embroidery needle

Sizes

This pattern comes in two sizes. The small size is about 18½in/47cm around the circumference and the large size 20in/51cm. Measure around your head to find out which size you need

Note: if you are knitting the larger size, follow the instructions in round brackets, which come second. For example, *Cast on 66 (78) stitches* means for the smaller size cast on 66 stitches, for the larger size cast on 78 stitches.

Gauge (tension)

14 sts and 18 rows in stockinette (stocking) stitch to a 4-in (10-cm) square on US 9 (5.5mm) needles.

Abbreviations

k knit
k2tog knit 2 stitches together
p purl
p2sso pass 2 slipped stitches over
p2tog purl 2 stitches together
rep repeat
RS right side
sl slip
st(s) stitches
st st stockinette (stocking) stitch
WS wrong side
[ ] work the stitches inside the brackets the number of times it says after the brackets

Techniques

Shaping (see pages 14–15)

Making pompoms (see page 20)

Sewing up (see page 19)

Sewing on buttons (see page 20)

Embroidery stitches (see page 22)

1

For the small size
Cast on 66 sts in gray.
Row 1: K2, [p2, k2] to end.
Row 2: P2, [k2, p2] to end.
Rep rows 1–2 once more.
Work 18 rows in st st beg with a k row.

For the large size
Cast on 72 sts in gray.
Row 1: [K2, p2] to end.
Rep row 1, 3 times more.
Work 22 rows in st st beg with a k row.
Next row: K5, [k2tog, k10] 5 times, k2tog, k5.
(66 sts)
Next row: Purl.

Carry on the same for both sizes
Next row: K4, [sl2, k1, p2sso, k8] 5 times, sl2, k1, p2sso, k4.
(54 sts)
Next row: Purl.
Next row: K3, [sl2, k1, p2sso, k6] 5 times, sl2, k1, p2sso, k3.
(42 sts)
Next row: Purl.

Next row: K2, [sl2, k1, p2sso, k4] 5 times, sl2, k1, p2sso, k2. *(30 sts)*
Next row: Purl.
Next row: K1, [sl2, k1, p2sso, k2] 5 times, sl2, k1, p2sso, k1. *(18 sts)*
Next row: [P2tog] to end. *(9 sts)*
Break yarn leaving a long tail. Thread yarn tail through rem sts, pull up tightly, and secure.

2 **Make the ears (make 2)**
Using pompom maker or cardboard circles and gray yarn, make two pompoms (see page 20). When you finish off the pompom, by winding yarn around the center and tying a knot, leave one long tail of yarn for attaching the ears to the hat.

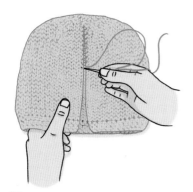

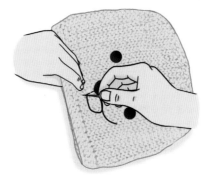

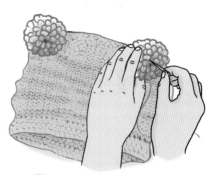

3 **Make up the hat**
Join the back seam of the hat using flat stitch (see page 19).

4 **Add the eyes and nose**
Sew the buttons in place for the eyes (see page 20), using the photograph as a guide. Using black yarn, work a coil in chain stitch (see page 22) for the nose and add a vertical straight stitch (see page 22) at the bottom of the nose.

5 **Add the ears**
Thread a needle on one of the long yarn tails of a pompom ear and use it to sew the ear into position. Repeat for the other ear. Weave in all loose ends.

Koala Book Cozy

Koalas are adorable creatures, and now you can knit one of your very own to keep the book you are reading clean and safe in your school bag or around the house. You will probably find that once you've knitted one of these cozies, your book-loving friends will be asking for one too!

You will need

Drops Air (70% alpaca, 23% polyamide, 7% wool; 142yd/130m per 1¾oz/50g ball) worsted (Aran) yarn:
  1 ball each in shades:
  04 Medium Grey and
  01 Off-White

Small amount of light worsted (DK) yarn in black

A handful of fiberfill toy stuffing

2 x ⅜in (8mm) black dome buttons

1 x ½in (11mm) snap fastener

US 6 (4mm) and US 2/3 (3mm) knitting needles

Yarn sewing needle

Large-eyed embroidery needle

Gauge (tension)

19 sts and 27 rows in stockinette (stocking) stitch to a 4-in (10-cm) square on US 6 (4mm) needles.

Measurements

The cozy is designed to fit a standard size paperback book, measuring approx. 5 x 7¾in (13 x 19.5cm) and about 1in (2.5cm) thick. The finished cozy measures 6 x 9in (15 x 23cm).

Abbreviations

inc increase
k knit
k2tog knit 2 stitches together
p purl
p2tog purl 2 stitches together
rep repeat
ssk slip slip knit
st(s) stitches
st st stockinette (stocking) stitch

Techniques

Joining in a new color (see page 16)

Shaping (see pages 14–15)

Sewing up (see page 19)

Embroidery stitches (see page 22)

Sewing on buttons (see page 20)

 Make the front of the cozy
Using US 6 (4mm) needles, cast on 30 sts in gray yarn.
Beg with a k row, work 22 rows in st st.
Break the gray yarn and join in the white.
Rows 23–58: Beg with a k row, work 36 rows in st st.
Row 59: [K1, p1] to end.
Rep row 59, 3 times more.
Bind (cast) off.

 Make the back of the cozy
Using US 6 (4mm) needles, cast on 30 sts in gray yarn.
Beg with a k row, work 62 rows in st st.
Bind (cast) off.

 Make the head (make 2)
Using US 6 (4mm) needles, cast on 27 sts in gray yarn.
Beg with a k row, work 18 rows in st st.
Row 19: K2, k2tog, k to last 4 sts, ssk, k2. *(25 sts)*
Row 20: Purl.
Row 21: K2, k2tog, k to last 4 sts, ssk, k2. *(23 sts)*
Row 22: P2tog, p to last 2 sts, p2tog. *(21 sts)*
Rep last 2 rows twice more. *(13 sts)*
Bind (cast) off.

 Make the arms (make 2)
Using US 6 (4mm) needles, cast on 12 sts in gray yarn.
Beg with a k row, work 12 rows in st st.
Row 13: [K2tog] to end. *(6 sts)*
Break yarn, thread through rem sts, and pull up tightly.

Make the ears (make 2)
Using US 6 (4mm) needles, cast on 14 sts in gray yarn.
Beg with a k row, work 6 rows in st st.
Row 7: [K2tog] to end. *(7 sts)*
Break yarn, thread through rem sts, and pull up tightly.

6 Make the nose

Using US 2/3 (3mm) needles, cast on 5 sts in black yarn.

Row 1: Inc, k to last 2 sts, inc, k1. *(7 sts)*
Row 2: Purl.
Rep rows 1–2 once more. *(9 sts)*
Row 5: Knit.
Row 6: Purl.
Row 7: K1, k2tog, k3, ssk, k1. *(7 sts)*
Row 8: Purl.
Row 9: K1, k2tog, k1, ssk, k1. *(5 sts)*
Row 10: P2tog, p1, p2tog. *(3 sts)*
Row 11: K3tog. *(1 st)*
Fasten off.

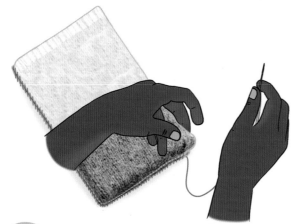

7 Join the body pieces

Join the main front and back pieces together at the base and sides using flat stitch (see page 19).

8 Attach the head

Join the two head pieces together. First with right sides together, oversew (see page 19) around the curved chin of the koala. Now turn the head the right way round—wrong sides together—and stitch the straight sides and top of the head using flat stitch. Oversew the head in position on the top of the body back.

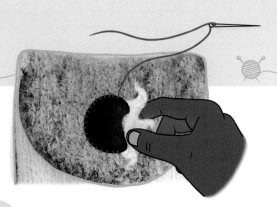

9   Add the nose
Oversew the nose in place, stuffing it lightly as you go. To make the outside edge of the nose really neat, work a line of chain stitch around it (see page 22) using black yarn.

10   Add the arms
Join the arm seams using flat stitch. Sew the arms in place on the side seams and work some straight stitches (see page 22) in black to secure the arms on the tummy, making the stitches look like claws.

11   Add the ears and eyes
Sew the seams on the ears using flat stitch (see page 19), stuff them lightly, and secure in place using the photo as a guide. Sew the button eyes in position (see page 20).

12   Sew on the snap fastener
Sew the snap fastener in position (see page 20) on the underneath part of the head. Fold the flap down and make a tiny pen mark to show where to sew on the other side of the fastener, on the body front. Sew it into position. Weave in all loose ends.

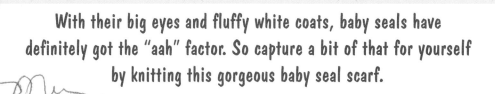

Seal Pup Scarf

With their big eyes and fluffy white coats, baby seals have definitely got the "aah" factor. So capture a bit of that for yourself by knitting this gorgeous baby seal scarf.

You will need

Rico Essentials Alpaca Blend Chunky (50% acrylic, 30% wool, 20% alpaca; 98yd/90m per 1¾oz/50g ball) bulky (chunky) yarn:
  2 balls in shade 001 Cream

Willow & Lark Plume (70% mohair, 30% silk; 230yd/210m per ¾oz/25g ball) lace weight yarn:
  1 ball in shade 301 Milk (cream)

Small amount of black light worsted (DK) yarn

US 10½ (6.5mm) knitting needles

4 x stitch markers or small safety pins

Yarn sewing needle

Large-eyed embroidery needle

Gauge (tension)

11 sts and 16 rows in stockinette (stocking) stitch to a 4-in (10-cm) square on US 10½ (6.5mm) needles using both yarns held together.

Measurements

The finished scarf is 38in (97cm) long.

Abbreviations

inc increase
k knit
k2tog knit 2 stitches together
m1 make 1 stitch
p purl
rep repeat
RS right side
sl slip
ssk slip slip knit
st st stockinette (stocking) stitch
st(s) stitch(es)
WS wrong side
* work instructions after or between asterisks (stars) as directed in the pattern

Techniques

Knitting with two yarns held together (see page 13)

Shaping (see pages 14–15)

Embroidery stitches (see page 22)

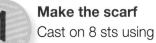

1 **Make the scarf**
Cast on 8 sts using the cream yarns held together.
Row 1: Inc, k to last 2 sts, inc, k1. *(10 sts)*
Row 2: Knit.
Row 3: K2, m1, k to last 2 sts, m1, k2. *(12 sts)*
Row 4: K2, p to last 2 sts, k2.
Rep rows 3–4, 5 times more. *(22 sts)*
Row 15: Knit.
Row 16: K2, p to last 2 sts, k2.
Rep rows 15–16, 6 times more,

placing a stitch marker or small safety pin at each end of row 28.
Rep rows 15–16, 6 times more.
Row 41: K2, ssk, k to last 4 sts, k2tog, k2. *(20 sts)*
Row 42: K2, p to last 2 sts, k2.
Row 43: Knit.
Row 44: K2, p to last 2 sts, k2.
Rep rows 43–44 twice more, placing a stitch marker or small safety pin at each end of row 48.
Rep rows 43–44, 34 times more.
Row 117: K2, ssk, k to last 4 sts, k2tog, k2. *(18 sts)*
Row 118: K2, p to last 2 sts, k2.

Row 119: Knit.
Row 120: K2, p to last 2 sts, k2.
Rep rows 119–120, 8 times more.
Row 137: K2, m1, k to last 2 sts, m1, k2. *(20 sts)*
Now shape the tail which has two separate flippers.
Row 138: K2, p6, k2, but don't knit the rest of the row. Turn and work on these 10 stitches only to make the first flipper. The other stitches remain on the needle but you don't knit them.
Next row: Knit.
Next row: K2, p to last 2 sts, k2.

Next row: Knit to last 2 sts, m1, k2. *(11 sts)*
Next row: K2, p to last 2 sts, k2.
Next row: Knit.
Next row: K2, p to last 2 sts, k2.
Rep last 4 rows once more.
(12 sts)
*__Next row:__ K2, ssk, k to last 4 sts, k2tog, k2. *(10 sts)*
Next row: K2, p to last 2 sts, k2.
Rep last 2 rows once more.
(8 sts)
Next row: K2, ssk, k2tog, k2.
(6 sts)
Next row: Ssk, k2, k2tog. *(4 sts)*
Next row: Ssk, k2tog. *(2 sts)*
Next row: K2tog. *(1 st)*
Break yarn and fasten off.

Now for the second flipper.
Rejoin yarn to the remaining
10 stitches left on your needle on
WS of work.
Next row: K2, p to last 2 sts, k2.
Next row: Knit.
Next row: K2, p to last 2 sts, k2.
Next row: K2, m1, k to end.
(11 sts)

Next row: K2, p to last 2 sts, k2.
Next row: Knit.
Next row: K2, p to last 2 sts, k2.
Rep last 4 rows once more.
*(12 sts)*__
Rep from * to **.

2 Make the front flippers

With RS facing, pick up and k 14 sts on one edge between the marker nearest the face and the marker nearest the tail.

Row 2: K2, p to last 2 sts, k2.

Row 3: K2, k2tog, k to last 2 sts, m1, k2.

Row 4: K2, p to last 2 sts, k2. Rep rows 2–3 twice more.

Row 9: K2, k2tog, k to end. *(13 sts)*

Row 10: K2, p to last 2 sts, k2. Rep rows 9–10 once more. *(12 sts)*

Row 13: K2, ssk, k to last 4 sts, k2tog, k2. *(10 sts)*

Row 14: K2, p to last 2 sts, k2.

Row 15: K1, ssk, k to last 3 sts, k2tog, k1. *(8 sts)*

Row 16: K1, ssk, k2, k2tog, k1. *(6 sts)*

Row 17: Ssk, k2, k2tog. *(4 sts)* Bind (cast) off.

With RS facing, pick up and k14 sts on the other edge between the marker nearest the tail and the marker nearest the face.

Row 2: K2, p to last 2 sts, k2.

Row 3: K2, m1, k to last 4 sts, k2tog, k2.

Row 4: K2, p to last 2 sts, k2. Rep rows 2–3 twice more.

Row 9: Knit to last 4 sts, ssk, k2. *(13 sts)*

Row 10: K2, p to last 2 sts, k2. Rep rows 9–10 once more. *(12 sts)*

Rep from * to end to complete the second flipper.

3 Embroider the face

Using black yarn, work two coils of chain stitch (see page 22) for the eyes and a rounded triangular shape for the nose.

4 Add the details

Using a separated strand of black yarn, work a few straight stitches (see page 22) for the whiskers around the nose and on the eyebrows. Weave in all loose ends.

Tropical Frog Scarf

How can anyone resist all the beautiful colors of tropical frogs? Copy the colors of a real species, or make up your own, as we have. I bet you have never seen a stripy bug-eyed frog like this one in your pond! Go wild with tropical colors to design your very own frog scarf.

You will need

Katia Maxi Merino (55% merino, 45% acrylic; 71yd/125m per 3½oz/100g ball) bulky (chunky) yarn:
  2 balls in shade 018 (green)
  1 ball in shade 033 (blue)

Small amount of off-white light worsted (DK) yarn

Small amount of black light worsted (DK) yarn

A handful of fiberfill toy stuffing

US 9 (5.5mm) knitting needles

Yarn sewing needle

Large-eyed embroidery needle

Gauge (tension)

13 sts and 18 rows in stockinette (stocking) stitch to a 4-in (10-cm) square on US 9 (5.5mm) needles.

Measurements

Scarf is 51in (130cm) long.

Abbreviations

inc increase
k knit
k2tog knit 2 stitches together
m1 make 1 stitch
psso pass slipped stitch over
rem remaining
sl slip
ssk slip slip knit
st(s) stitch(es)
st st stockinette (stocking) stitch

[] knit the stitches inside the square brackets as many times as the instructions after the brackets tell you

Techniques

Knitting with two yarns held together (see page 13)

Shaping (see pages 14–15)

Carrying yarn up the side of the work (see page 16)

Sewing up (see page 19)

Embroidery stitches (see page 22)

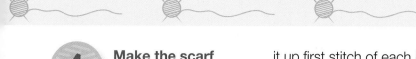

 1 **Make the scarf**
Cast on 10 sts in
green yarn.
Row 1: Inc, k to last st, inc, k1.
(12 sts)
Row 2: Purl.
Row 3: K1, m1, k to last st, m1,
k1. *(14 sts)*
Row 4: Purl.
Rep rows 3–4, 5 times more.
(24 sts)
Beg with a k row, work 8 rows
in st st.
Row 23: K2, ssk, k to last 4 sts,
k2tog, k2. *(22 sts)*
Row 24: Purl.
Row 25: K2, ssk, k to last 4 sts,
k2tog, k2. *(20 sts)*
Row 26: Knit.
Row 27: K3, p to last 3 sts, k3.
Rep rows 26–27 twice more.
Leave green yarn at side
(weaving it up first stitch of each
k row until needed again) and join
in blue.
Row 32: Knit.
Row 33: K3, p to last 3 sts, k3.
Leave blue yarn at side (weaving

it up first stitch of each k row until
needed again) and use green.
Rep rows 26–33 (last 8 rows),
20 times more.
Break blue yarn and work
remainder of scarf in green.
Row 194: Knit.
Row 195: K3, p to last 3 sts, k3.
Rep rows 194–195 twice more.
Knit 6 rows.
Now shape the back legs so
you have two separate legs
hanging down.
Row 206: K7, bind (cast) off 6 sts
(to leave a gap between the legs),
k to end.
Work on last group of 7 stitches
you have just worked. When you
reach the gap, turn and don't knit
the rest of the row. The other
stitches remain on the needle but
you don't knit them.
*Knit 11 rows.
Beg with a k row, work 22 rows
in st st.
Shape foot into long separate
toes.
Next row: K2, turn and work on

these 2 sts only, leaving rem sts
on needle.
Beg with a p row, work 5 rows
in st st.
Next row: K2tog, [pick up and k
1 st from row ends, bind/cast off
1 st] 4 times (1 st rem on needle),
k1, bind (cast) off 1 st, k2. Turn
and work on these 3 sts only,
leaving rem sts on needle.
Beg with a p row, work 5 rows
in st st.
Next row: Sl1, k2tog, psso, [pick
up and k 1 st from row ends, bind/
cast off 1 st] 4 times (1 st rem on
needle), k1, bind (cast) off 1 st, k1.
Turn and work on these 2 sts only,
leaving rem sts on needle.
Beg with a p row, work 5 rows
in st st.
Next row: K2tog, [pick up and k
1 st from row ends, bind/cast off
1 st] 4 times. (1 st rem on needle.)
Break yarn and fasten off.
Rejoin green to second group of
sts on needle on WS of work and
rep from * to end.

 2 **Make the front leg
(make 2)**
Cast on 7 sts in green.
Beg with a k row, work 42 rows
in st st.
Shape foot as for back legs.

 3 **Make the face**
Cast on 10 sts in green.
Row 1: Inc, k to last st,
inc, k1. *(12 sts)*
Row 2: Purl.
Row 3: K1, m1, k to last st, m1,
k1. *(14 sts)*
Row 4: Purl.
Rep rows 3–4, 5 times more.
(24 sts)

Beg with a k row, work 8 rows
in st st.
Row 23: K2, ssk, k to last 4 sts,
k2tog, k2. *(22 sts)*
Row 24: Purl.
Row 25: K2, ssk, k to last 4 sts,
k2tog, k2. *(20 sts)*
Row 26: Purl.
Bind (cast) off.

4 **Make the eye hoods (make 2)**
Cast on 3 sts in green.
Row 1: [Inc] 3 times. *(6 sts)*
Row 2: Knit.
Row 3: K1, [m1, k1] to end. *(11 sts)*
Row 4: Knit.
Bind (cast) off.

5 **Make the eyeballs (make 2)**
Cast on 4 sts using off-white yarn double.
Row 1: [Inc] 4 times. *(8 sts)*
Row 2: Purl.
Row 3: K1, [m1, k1] to end. *(15 sts)*
Row 4: Purl.
Row 5: [K2tog] 3 times, sl1, k2tog, psso, [ssk] 3 times. *(7 sts)*
Break yarn, thread it through rem sts, and pull up securely.

6 **Attach the eyes**
Sew the eye hoods in place on the face so that the bound- (cast-) off edges form the outer rim of the eye hood. Join the side seam of the eyeballs using flat stitch (see page 19), stuffing lightly as you go. Place the eyeballs in the eye hoods. Stitch in place along the part of the eyeball that meets the main scarf and along the outer rim of the eye hood.

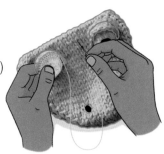

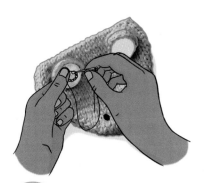

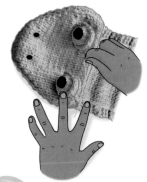

7 **Embroider the details**
Using black yarn, work the center of the eye in chain stitch (see page 22). Work two small circles of chain stitch in black yarn for the nostrils.

8 **Attach the face**
Place the face on the head part of the main scarf so that the right sides are together. Oversew (see page 19) the side and lower seams. Turn the head the right way out and sew the top edge in place using flat stitch.

9 **Add the legs**
Oversew the front legs in place underneath the head, where the head meets the main part of the scarf. Weave in all loose ends.

Reindeer Hat

When it's snowy outside and you need to keep your head warm, there's nothing cozier than a knitted reindeer hat topped with a couple of perky antlers. Knit him with a red nose like we've done here, or if you wish, you could use a pompom for his nose instead. Remember, reindeers are not just for Christmas!

You will need

Katia Merino 100% (100% merino wool;111 yd/102m per1¾oz/50g ball) light worsted (DK) yarn:
2 balls in shade 501 (brown)
1 ball in shade 500 (beige)

Small amount of Debbie Bliss Rialto DK in shade 12 Red

Small amounts of Sirdar Country Style DK in shade 417 Black and shade 411 Cream

Small amount of fiberfill toy stuffing

Sizes US 9 (5.5mm) and US 3 (3.25mm) knitting needles

US 7 (4.5mm) crochet hook or hook of similar size

Yarn sewing needle

Large-eyed embroidery needle

2 x stitch markers or small safety pins

Sizes

This pattern comes in two sizes: a smaller size to fit 3–10 years and a larger size to fit 11 years and over.

Note: if you are knitting the larger size, follow the instructions in round brackets, which come second. For example, *Cast on 66 (78) stitches* means for the smaller size cast on 66 stitches, for the larger size cast on 78 stitches.

Actual measurements

Approx 17½in/44cm (19in/48cm) circumference

Gauge (tension)

15 sts and 24 rows to 4-in (10-cm) square over stockinette (stocking) stitch using yarn double on US 9 (5.5mm) needles.

Abbreviations

inc increase
k knit
k2tog knit 2 stitches together
LH left hand
m1 make 1 stitch
p purl
psso pass the slipped stitch over
p2tog purl 2 stitches together
pwise purlwise
rep repeat
RH right hand
RS right side
sl slip
ssk slip slip knit
st(s) stitches
st st stockinette (stocking) stitch
WS wrong side
[ ] work the stitches inside the brackets the number of times it says after the brackets

Techniques

Shaping (see pages 14–15)

Knitting with two yarns held together (see page 13)

Picking up stitches (see page 18)

Sewing up (see page 19)

Embroidery stitches (see page 22)

Crochet techniques (see page 21)

1 Make the hat (make 1)

Using US 9 (5.5 mm) needles and brown yarn, cast on 66 (72) sts using yarn double. Place a small safety pin marker at 22nd (24th) st in from each edge. Work 22(26) rows in st st beg with a k row.

Large size only:

Row 27: K5, [k2tog, k10] 5 times, k2tog, k5. *(66 sts)*

Row 28: Purl.

Both sizes:

Next row: K4, [sl1, k2tog, psso, k8] 5 times, sl1, k2tog, psso, k4. *(54 sts)*

Next and every WS row until stated otherwise: P.

Next RS row: K3, [sl1, k2tog, psso, k6] 5 times, sl1, k2tog, psso, k3. *(42 sts)*

Next RS row: K2, [sl1, k2tog, psso, k4] 5 times, sl1, k2tog, psso, k2. *(30 sts)*

Next RS row: K1, [sl1, k2tog, psso, k2] 5 times, sl1, k2tog, psso, k1. *(18 sts)*

Next row (WS): P2tog to end. *(9 sts)*

Break yarn leaving a long tail. Thread yarn tail through rem sts, pull up tightly, and secure.

For the shaped bottom of the hat, you work one side at a time. With RS of work facing and using doubled strand of brown yarn, pick up and k 22 (24) sts across lower edge from RH edge toward first safety pin marker.

Work 3 rows in st st beg with a p row.

Next row: K to last 2 sts, ssk. *(21/23 sts)*

Next row: P2tog, p to end. *(20/22 sts)*

Rep last 2 rows 2(3) times more. *(16 sts)*

Bind (cast) off.

With RS of work facing and using doubled strand of brown yarn, pick up and k 22 (24) sts across lower edge from second safety pin marker to LH edge.

Work 3 rows in st st beg with a p row.

Next row: K2tog, k to end. *(21/23 sts)*

Next row: P to last 2 sts, p2tog. *(20/22 sts)*

Rep last 2 rows twice (3 times) more. *(16 sts)*

Bind (cast) off.

2 Make the ears (make 4 pieces)

Using US 9 (5.5mm) needles and brown yarn, cast on 10 sts using yarn double. Work 8 rows in st st beg with a k row.

Row 9: K1, k2tog, k to last 3 sts, ssk, k1. *(8 sts)*
Row 10: Purl.
Rep Rows 9–10 once more. *(6 sts)*
Row 13: K1, k2tog, ssk, k1. *(4 sts)*

Row 14: [P2tog] twice. *(2 sts)*
Row 15: K2tog. *(1 st)*
Break yarn and pull through rem st.

3 Make the antlers (make 4 pieces)

Using US 3 (3.25 mm) needles and beige yarn, cast on 5 sts.
Work 8 rows in st st beg with a k row.
Row 9: Inc, k2, inc1, k1. *(7 sts)*
Row 10: Inc1 pwise, p to last 2 sts, inc1 pwise, p1. *(9 sts)*
Row 11: Inc1, k to last 2 sts, inc1, k1. *(11 sts)*
Row 12: Purl.
Row 13: K4, m1, k3, m1, k4. *(13 sts)*
Now shape the branches of the antlers by splitting your knitting into three parts.
Row 14: P4 but don't knit the rest of the row. Turn and work on

these 4 stitches only, leaving the remaining stitches on the needle. Work 2 rows in st st beg with a k row.
Row 17: K2tog, ssk. *(2 sts)*
Row 18: P2tog. *(1 st)*
Break yarn and pull through remaining stitches.

Now knit the next branch of the antler. Rejoin yarn to the remaining stitches on WS of work.
Next row: P5, turn and work on these 5 sts only, leaving rem sts on needle.
Work 5 rows in st st beg with a k row.
Next row: P2tog, p1, p2tog. *(3 sts)*

Next row: Sl1, k2tog, psso. *(1 st)*
Break yarn and pull through rem st.

This is the last branch. Rejoin yarn to rem 4 sts on WS of work. Work 3 rows in st st beg with a p row.
Next row: K2tog, ssk. *(2 sts)*
Next row: P2tog. *(1 st)*
Break yarn and pull through rem st.

4 Make the nose (make 1)

Using US 3 (3.25mm) needles and red yarn, cast on 8 sts.
Row 1: Inc, k to last 2 sts, inc, k1. *(10 sts)*

Row 2: Inc pwise, p to last 2 sts, inc pwise, p1. *(12 sts)*
Row 3: Inc1, k to last 2 sts, inc, k1. *(14 sts)*
Work 3 rows in st st beg with a p row.
Row 7: K1, k2tog, k to last 3 sts, ssk, k1. *(12 sts)*

Row 8: P2tog, p to last 2 sts, p2tog. *(10 sts)*
Row 9: K1, k2tog, k to last 3 sts, ssk, k1. *(8 sts)*
Bind (cast) off pwise.

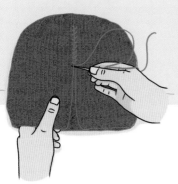

 5 **Make up the hat**
Join back seam of hat using flat stitch (see page 19).

6 **Adding the ears**
Place two ear pieces right sides together. Oversew (see page 19) the sides. Turn the ear right sides out and oversew the lower edge. Make the second ear in the same way. Fold the ears in half lengthwise and stitch in place along the short folded edge, so the folded edge is parallel to the lower edge of the hat.

7 **Adding the antlers**
Place two antler pieces wrong sides together. Oversew around the edges, leaving the lower edge open, and stuff very lightly with the toy stuffing, using a pencil to push the stuffing into the points of the antler. Oversew the bottom edges together. Make the second antler in the same way. Stitch the antlers in position.

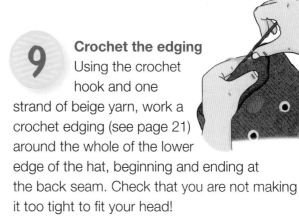

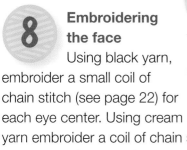

8 **Embroidering the face**
Using black yarn, embroider a small coil of chain stitch (see page 22) for each eye center. Using cream yarn embroider a coil of chain stitch around each eye center. Oversew the nose in place.

9 **Crochet the edging**
Using the crochet hook and one strand of beige yarn, work a crochet edging (see page 21) around the whole of the lower edge of the hat, beginning and ending at the back seam. Check that you are not making it too tight to fit your head!

Aardvark

Aardvarks are weird, long-nosed, termite-eating African mammals. This little knitted one would make a great companion for anyone who finds teddies and bunnies... well, just a little too obvious and cute. This one is knitted in a mauve wool-mix yarn, but you could knit one in any color you want.

You will need

Sirdar Country Style DK (40% nylon, 30% wool, 30% acrylic; 170yd/155m per 1¾oz/50g ball) light worsted (DK) yarn:
  1 ball in shade 615 Purple Sage

Very small amounts of black and white light worsted (DK) yarn

A few handfuls of fiberfill toy stuffing

US 3 (3.25mm) knitting needles

2 x stitch markers or small safety pins

Yarn sewing needle

Large-eyed embroidery needle

Gauge (tension)

24 sts and 32 rows in stockinette (stocking) stitch to a 4-in (10-cm) square on US 3 (3.25mm) needles.

Measurements

The finished toy is 8in (20cm) long (excluding tail).

Abbreviations

k knit
k2tog knit 2 stitches together
m1 make 1 stitch
p purl
p3tog purl 3 stitches together
pwise purlwise
rem remaining
st(s) stitch(es)
st st stockinette (stocking) stitch
[ ] knit the stitches inside the square brackets as many times as the instructions after the brackets tell you
* work instructions after or between asterisks (stars) as directed in the pattern

Techniques

Shaping (see pages 14–15)

Sewing up (see page 19)

Embroidery stitches (see page 22)

---

1 **Make the first side of the aardvark**
Cast on 6 sts for front leg.
Beg with a k row, work 8 rows in st st.
Row 9: K1, m1, k to last st, m1, k1. *(8 sts)*
Row 10: Purl.
Rep rows 9–10 once more. *(10 sts)*

Break yarn and leave sts on needle.
On needle with sts, cast on another 6 sts for back leg.
Beg with a k row, work 6 rows in st st.
Row 7: K to last st, m1, k1. *(7 sts)*
Row 8: Purl.
Rep rows 7–8 once more. *(8 sts)*

Next row: Join the back and front legs onto the body. K8 sts from back leg, turn work and cast on 16 sts, turn work back and k9 from front leg, m1, k1. *(35 sts)*
Next row: Purl.
Next row: K to last 2 sts, m1, k1, m1, k1. *(37 sts)*
Next row: Purl.*

Rep last 2 rows twice more. *(41 sts)*

Next row: K to last 2 sts, m1, k1, m1, k1. *(43 sts)*

Next row: Cast on 12 sts at beg of row, p to end. *(55 sts)*

Beg with a k row, work 5 rows in st st.

Next row: Bind (cast) off 4 sts pwise, p to end. *(51 sts)*

Next row: K2, k2tog, k to end. *(50 sts)*

Next row: Bind (cast) off 4 sts pwise, p to end. *(46 sts)*

Next row: Knit.

Next row: Bind (cast) off 4 sts pwise, p to end. *(42 sts)*

Next row: K2, k2tog, k to end. *(41 sts)*

Next row: Bind (cast) off 4 sts pwise, p to end. *(37 sts)*

Next row: K2, k2tog, k to end. *(36 sts)*

Next row: Bind (cast) off 4 sts pwise, p to end. *(32 sts)*

Next row: Bind (cast) off 4 sts, k to end. *(28 sts)*

Next row: Bind (cast) off 4 sts pwise, p to end. *(24 sts)*

Bind (cast) off.

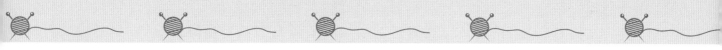

2 **Make the second side of the aardvark**
Cast on 6 sts for back leg.

Beg with a k row, work 6 rows in st st.

Row 7: K1, m1, k to end. *(7 sts)*

Row 8: Purl.

Rep rows 7–8 once more. *(8 sts)*

Break yarn and leave sts on needle.

On needle with sts, cast on another 6 sts for front leg.

Beg with a k row, work 8 rows in st st.

Row 9: K1, m1, k to last st, m1, k1. *(8 sts)*

Row 10: Purl.

Rep last 2 rows once more. *(10 sts)*

Next row: K1, m1, k rem 9 sts from front leg, turn work and cast on 16 sts, turn work back and k8 from back leg. *(35 sts)*

Next row: Purl.

Next row: [K1, m1] twice, k to end. *(37 sts)*

Next row: Purl.

Rep last 2 rows twice more. *(41 sts)*

Next row: [K1, m1] twice, k to end. *(43 sts)*

Next row: Purl.

Next row: Cast on 12 sts at beg of row, k to end. *(55 sts)*

Beg with a p row, work 5 rows in st st.

Next row: Bind (cast) off 4 sts, k to last 4 sts, ssk, k2. *(50 sts)*

Next row: Purl.

Next row: Bind (cast) off 4 sts, k to end. *(46 sts)*

Next row: Purl.

Next row: Bind (cast) off 4 sts, k to last 4 sts, ssk, k2. *(41 sts)*

Next row: Purl.

Next row: Bind (cast) off 4 sts, k to last 4 sts, ssk, k2. *(36 sts)*

Next row: Bind (cast) off 4 sts pwise, p to end. *(32 sts)*

Next row: Bind (cast) off 4 sts, k to end. *(28 sts)*

Next row: Bind (cast) off 4 sts pwise, p to end. *(24 sts)*

Bind (cast) off.

3 **Make the gusset**
This is the part that goes underneath the aardvark to make it 3D. You begin with the insides of two legs, then knit the tummy, and then the knitting divides again so that you are knitting the insides of the other two legs.

Work as for first side to *.

Next row: K to last 2 sts, m1, k1, m1, k1. *(39 sts)*

Next row: Purl.

Next row: K to last 5 sts, [k2tog] twice, k1. *(37 sts)*

Next row: Purl.

Rep last 2 rows once more. *(35 sts)*

Next row: K8, turn, work on these 8 sts only, leaving rem sts on needle.

Next row: P2tog, p to end. *(7 sts)*

Next row: Knit.

Next row: P2tog, p to end. *(6 sts)*

Beg with a k row, work 6 rows in st st.

Bind (cast) off.

Rejoin yarn to rem 27 sts on RS of work.

Next row: Bind (cast) off 16 sts, k to last 3 sts, k2tog, k1. *(10 sts)*

Next row: P2tog, p to last 2 sts, p2tog. *(8 sts)*

Next row: Knit.

Next row: P2tog, p to last 2 sts, p2tog. *(6 sts)*

Beg with a k row, work 8 rows in st st.

Bind (cast) off.

4 Make the tail

Cast on 12 sts.

Beg with a k row, work 8 rows in st st.

Row 9: K1, k2tog, k to last 3 sts, ssk, k1. *(10 sts)*

Beg with a p row, work 5 rows in st st.

Rep rows 9–14 (last 6 rows) once more. *(8 sts)*

Row 21: K1, k2tog, k to last 2 sts, ssk, k1. *(6 sts)*

Beg with a p row, work 3 rows in st st.

Row 25: K1, k2tog, ssk, k1. *(4 sts)*

Row 26: [P2tog] twice. *(2 sts)*

Row 27: K2tog. *(1 st)*

Fasten off.

5 Make the ears (make 4)

Cast on 5 sts.

Beg with a k row, work 8 rows in st st.

Row 9: Ssk, k1, k2tog. *(3 sts)*

Row 10: P3tog. *(1 st)*

Fasten off.

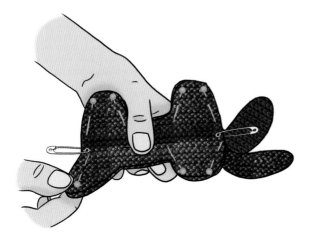

6 Join the pieces

Fold the gusset piece in half lengthwise and mark each end of the fold with a stitch marker or small safety pin. This will mark the center line of the gusset—one half will be sewn to one side of the lower part of the body; the other half will be sewn to the second side of the body. Pin the gusset in position, so the right sides of your work are together. Oversew (see page 19) or backstitch (see page 19) in place.

7 Stuff the aardvark

Oversew or backstitch the remaining parts of the body together leaving a gap in the top for turning and stuffing. Make sure that you stitch securely at the ends of the gusset where you begin stitching the two halves of the aardvark together so that you don't have a little hole here. Turn and stuff. Use your finger or the wrong end of a pencil to push stuffing firmly into the nose and legs so it is smooth and plump and stands up well. Stitch the gap closed.

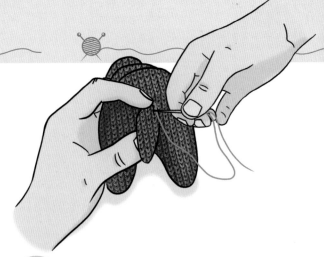

8 Add the tail
Sew the long seam of the tail using flat stitch (see page 19). Stuff lightly and oversew in position.

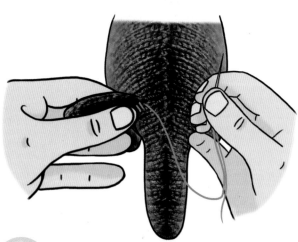

9 Add the ears
Place two ear pieces right sides together and oversew around the curved edges, leaving lower edges open. Repeat for the second ear. Turn the ears the right way out and sew in position, using the photo as a guide.

10 Embroider the eyes
Using black yarn, work two French knots (see page 22) for the eye centers. Cut a length of white yarn and pull off one strand. Use this to work a few coils of chain stitch (see page 22) around each eye center. Weave in all loose ends.

Suppliers

This is a list of some of the major suppliers of the yarns used in this book. For reasons of space, we cannot cover all stockists so please explore the local knitting shops and online stores in your own country. Please remember that from time to time companies will change the brands they supply or stock and will not always offer the full range. If you cannot find a particular yarn locally, there will usually be an excellent alternative and your local yarn store is the best place to ask about this, or visit www.yarnsub.com.

USA

KNITTING FEVER INC.
Online sales
www.knittingfever.com

LOVE KNITTING
Online sales
www.loveknitting.com

JO-ANN FABRIC AND CRAFT STORES
Retail stores and online
www.joann.com
Store locator on website

WEBS
www.yarn.com

LION BRAND YARNS
Online sales
www.lionbrand.com
Stockist locator on website (USA, Mexico, and Canada)

UK

LOVE KNITTING
Online sales
www.loveknitting.com

DERAMORES
Online sales
www.deramores.com

JOHN LEWIS
Retail stores and online
www.johnlewis.com
Store locator on website.

LAUGHING HENS
Online sales
www.laughinghens.com
Tel: +44 (0) 1829 740903

Australia

BLACK SHEEP WOOL 'N' WARES
Retail store and online
www.blacksheepwool.com.au

SUNSPUN FINE YARNS
Retail store only (Canterbury, Victoria)
sunspun.com.au

Finding a yarn stockist in your country

The following websites will help you find stockists for these yarn brands in your country. Please note that not all brands or types of yarn will be available in all countries.

CASCADE YARNS
www.cascadeyarns.com

DROPS DESIGN
www.garnstudio.com

KING COLE
www.kingcole.com

PLYMOUTH YARN
www.plymouthyarn.com

RED HEART
www.redheart.co.uk
www.redheart.com

RICO DESIGN
www.rico-design.de

ROWAN YARNS
Tel: +44 (0) 1484 681881
www.knitrowan.com

SCHACHENMAYR
www.schachenmayr.com

SIRDAR (INC. SUBLIME)
Tel: +44 (0) 1924 231682
www.sirdar.co.uk

Index

Picture credits

Terry Benson, projects on pages 38, 41, 44, 48, 64, 67, 73, 78, 88,
  93, 100, 106, 112, 115, 122
Emma Mitchell, project on page 118
Penny Wincer, projects on pages 26, 29, 32, 35, 54, 56, 58, 60, 70,
  83, 90, 96, 103, 108